Unpacked Luggage

By

Chyvonne Thomas

United Book Publishing
ISBN: 979-8-218-71647-9
Edited by: United Book Publishing
Printed in the United States of America by United Book Publishing

Book Design Credit and Synopsis Credit: David Essiet of Akwa-Ibom, Nigeria (Essietdavidtritones1@gmail.com)

To schedule a group workshop or interview, send an email to unpackedluggageinfo@gmail.com or chyvonne60@gmail.com.

Social media Platforms: Facebook @Chyvonne Thomas. Website: www.plrmotivational.com

Dedications

I first give thanks to Christ Jesus; he is the reason I exist. I dedicate this book to my late mother, Linda G. Thomas. Your legacy travels with me every single day. Not many days go by without me thinking about the kind of person you were. I thank you for a lifelong feeling of unconditional love. You have shown me what it means to be a good woman of faith and believer of Christ Jesus.

I want to thank my New Life Ministries family of Edison, New Jersey. I thank you for your love and support through my continued journey in Christ.

To the entire "ThomasNation", my love for you overflows!

A special thanks to my sister Alicia and brother William Thomas... here comes another one! I thank you for supporting me in everything I do. To my younger siblings, Angela and Jordan-I love you from many miles away.

I dedicate this book to every person seeking Jesus Christ.

Contents

Intro

I heard the Lord speaking to my spirit for months before reluctantly grabbing my computer to translate each word into this document. The reluctance stemmed from the uprooting of emotions and re-visitation of past traumas that would arise to complete this assignment.

In the stillness, I sat quiet, allowing space and time for the Holy Spirit to complete a download of words destined to flow through me.

Drifts in between dreams engulfed by spontaneous stares carried me into an unfamiliar space. These moments soon morphed into peaceful encounters that embraced my existence. They became open invitations as I understood God was using these specific moments to gift me with manifestations, visions, and thoughts. I realized that God was spiritually taking me into a secret place to show me, ME!

God showed me the words, "Unpacked Luggage," my altar where I would leave my journey all between the pages.

Unpacked Luggage: a book that metaphorically drives in the hands of people across all genres of life. A transformative journey of faith and self-discovery! A deep personal narrative, which shares profound experiences of divine revelation! A look into how God illuminated my path and revealed his true light in my life.

While *"Unpacked Luggage"* narrates my travel to Christ Jesus, it also allows readers to self-reflect on their journey.

Welcome to *"Unpacked Luggage."*

Some names have been omitted to help keep the book's integrity intact.

The Manual

"I removed myself from my hiding place and greeted her without letting her know I had been a witness."

I'm going somewhere with this! Before getting a legal driver's license, we must study a driver's manual to pass the test in our specific state. By studying the manual, we learn about different laws, rules, orders, and formations for maneuvering a vehicle. But that's not the only way to learn about driving. For some, knowledge and influence about driving derive from being around others who drive. Some learn from playing video games or watching others drive as they ride as a passenger. To go a little further, some people just have an innate immunity. In other words, it's just in them.

As humans, we can learn both consciously and unconsciously. Learning consciously is reading and engaging in the learning process. We may read certain material and then test our skills to determine our level of mastery in that certain area. However, unconscious learning happens without awareness caused by patterns and habits.

As a child, I'm pretty sure I've also learned a few things regarding driving through patterns and routines. I knew better than to distract my mom while the car was moving.

And somehow understood that sitting in the front seat was like eating forbidden fruit. Unconsciously, my brain associated green with "go" and red with "stop," but I still didn't know the reasons for the signals.

In hindsight, the same thing happened to me regarding learning about Jesus Christ.

At a young age, I unconsciously knew the name

"Jesus," but I really didn't know the reason for him.

For me, Grandma Lillie spoke about Jesus all the time. She had so many good things to say about him. From what I could hear, it seemed like the two of them were really close friends. The one thing I couldn't understand was why he never visited her. I mean, everyone else came to visit her, but not Jesus. I can easily say that on any given day, Grandma Lillie had about ten people visiting her. This was in addition to her adult kids flowing in and out of the house. Grandma Lillie birthed thirteen children, and of those children, they birthed children. That's a lot of people, and I fell into the younger half of her children's-children.

Grandma Lillie owned a cozy candy box in the back pantry of her apartment in Potter's Crossing; the only projects built on the North side of Edison. This place housed a huge melting pot of black families who merged together to form a community during a time of redevelopment.

If I were to give you the history of Potter's Crossing, it would call for me to write another book. But I will say this: I bet anyone who came through Potter's Crossing can recall a story about my Grandma Lillie's candy box. Now, alongside my Grandma, we had Mrs. Adam; she was the lady who sold cupcakes and pickles, sometimes Chitlins. What a combination, I know, but as I can remember, anything they sold kept the neighborhood talking like the latest rumor.

As a kid, there was no better feeling than to hustle pennies and nickels from aunties, uncles, moms, and dads before taking that skip down to Grandma Lillie's house to buy candy.

I remember that candy box like yesterday. It was a tall metal locker heavily painted with a thick coat of blue. Similar to the old lockers at school, but this one had double doors that guarded itself with a big lock during her closed hours of operation.

The kids, including myself, would crowd outside her apartment, waiting for her genuine love for people to usher her into giving free candy away.

I didn't know it then, but I do know now that her candy box embodied more than just selling candy. This box filled with sweet treats and rich chocolates held a bigger purpose; it offered a divine exchange with God. It stood as a beacon of community and faith. It was a representation of Jesus' love for people.

We went to the box for candy but also left with some kind of reference about Jesus.

Oftentimes, my mother talked about Jesus too, but like Grandma Lillie, she never brought him around either. I just didn't get it.

As my memory takes me back to about 1985, I remember walking in on my mom and finding her talking to the ceiling. She was prostrated on her knees with her hands crossed, calling out Jesus, Jesus!

She hadn't noticed my quiet entry sneaking in from behind. Unsure of what was happening, I hid my slim figure by the wall to take a peek back at her. With much anticipation, I canvased the room with my little eyes only to discover that she was all alone. I wondered if maybe Jesus was in the closet or under the bed. Her voice gained more volume with every beckoning for him. Her call for him grew into a cry that almost blew my cover that I was present. Badly, I wanted to enter the room to help her find Jesus; however, the sight of what was happening held me captive in my hiding place.

I was thinking about the many times I've played hide-and-seek with my friends. They usually jumped out of their hiding place when they realized I couldn't find them. But Jesus was a relentless player; he wouldn't come out for nothing.

The setting grew more intense when she began to thank Jesus. I wondered why mom would thank Jesus when he hadn't come out yet. Eventually, her cries came to a halt, and silence took control of the room. I removed myself from my hiding place and greeted her without letting her know I had been a witness.

Another reference about Jesus came to me at my pop-pop Willie's funeral. The preacher said, "he is, God, Jesus, Lord and Savior..." from there, I knew Jesus had more than one name. On this same day, I was introduced to the word heaven. It seemed like heaven was a good place to go, especially because the pastor said pop-pop was in a better place and in the hands of the Lord.

I remember sitting close by, watching my older cousins cry while others danced uncontrolled where pop-pop was sleeping. While I still didn't understand who Jesus was, something innate told me that his physical state was not here like mine. He had to live somewhere in the sky. I gathered that wherever he was and whoever he was, he was good because the whole church thought so.

The first time I called on Jesus happened while watching my mother from her bedroom window of our projects, the same projects as Grandma Lillie's. She was having a conversation with an older white man when the conversation came to an abrupt stop with anger. I watched her walk at a fast pace across the street, heading back to our apartment. She was venting to a friend about the sudden loss of her job. From afar, I saw the tears falling from her face as she grew closer to me. Her voice trembled with worry as she began to talk to herself about how she would make ends meet to put food on the table. At that moment, I remembered her friend Jesus and asked him to help my mom feed us. A few weeks later, I watched her standing in the mirror, preparing for work. This is the same job she would later retire from. I let her know that I had asked Jesus for help, and in return – she gave a stare that let me know I had done something good.

A seed of faith had been planted here, but being so young, I really didn't understand it. And more seeds just like that were planted in my soil as I grew into my teenage years. I remember being gifted with my first bible from my mother's co-worker. Her friend placed the bible inside the car my mom gifted to me when I turned eighteen. *The inside of the cover read: To Chyvonne.*

My bible collected so much dust that occasionally, I'd swipe my hand across it to measure the time lapse since I last opened it. However, seeds were still being planted in me about Jesus, but unconsciously. Similar to how we breathe. We breathe unconsciously and automatically for physical life; that same analogy can be applied to our spiritual life. We ingest information unconsciously and automatically. However, at some point in our spiritual nature, we awaken in God's purpose to seek him with a conscious mind.

One might ponder, if that's true, how is it that some of us believe in different religions and worship gods other than Jesus Christ? I, too, have asked that same question during my travel to Christ.

Family structure and dynamics, demographic influences, and the lack of knowledge about Christ can be a reason. Free-will is also a main artery that supplies oxygen to false gods.

However, we all have an innate immunity when it comes to God. The spirit of Jesus lives in us; however, we have to apply conscious learning to awaken planted seeds.

The story of Jeremiah. While God had predestined plans for Jeremiah, his love for humanity did not force him.

Jesus' standard remains the same today. He does not force us. Sometimes, we shy away from God because we may feel inadequate, just like Jeremiah did initially, but God reassured him of his presence. He is waiting to do the same for us!

"Before I formed you in the womb, I knew you before you were born, I sanctified you; and I ordained you a prophet to the nations."
—(Jeremiah 1:5)

Waiting for us to awaken those seeds he planted in us since birth.

Crutch

And wait, I felt super-vindicated when "so-called Christians" talked about my sins while theirs danced in private spaces all night long.

"God knows my heart!" But wait – let me share another one with you, "I ain't hurting nobody!" These two statements protected me like guard dogs from anyone who came against my homosexual lifestyle. I had those words reserved at the tip of my tongue, ready to hiss at anyone who challenged me.

My defense mechanism was always locked and loaded. Those words encompassed a certain level of power and self-control over my life; I felt vindicated!

And wait, I felt super-vindicated when "so-called Christians" talked about my sins while theirs danced in private spaces all night long. I think those types of encounters gave me more reason to go deeper into the life I was living.

But first, let me unpack how homosexuality became a part of my life. Now, there's a lot of research and theory about where homosexuality derives from. While there is no "gay gene" proven in humans to this day, I will loosely add that scientists suggest that homosexuality is caused by a complex interplay of genetic, hormonal, and environmental influences.

Plenty of times, I've heard many people say they were born with same-sex attraction. While others may have experienced some trauma like molestation or even abuse to abandon heterosexuality. The reality is this; the list continues to increase in height– of why people engage in homosexuality.

My deep dive into homosexuality was not that complex. Do I feel like I was born gay? I would say no because, as a young kid, I didn't experience same-sex attraction. I experienced having healthy crushes on the opposite sex. Growing up, I had childhood boyfriends whom I liked while in middle school. I passed notes back and forth with boys just as other girls did. I even had a boyfriend in high school. However, I wasn't sexually active as some of my friends were, but I still liked them. Unfortunately, most of my boyfriends broke up with me after I refused to have sex as a teenager. But overall, sexuality was not a burden that weighed heavy on me. My concentration was sports. However, that's not the case for others. How many times have you heard stories about kids being as young as four and five feeling like they were gay? Or better yet, how many times have you witnessed a young boy behave in a very "sassy" way?

That wasn't my story. I sum my life of homosexuality up to being part persona, exploration, part space, and opportunity.

My persona! As a little girl, I hung around many of my boy cousins doing the same things they did. We built clubhouses, we worked on our bikes together, I played basketball with them, football...you name it, I was right there along with them. Meanwhile, my girl cousins were in the house playing with their cabbage patch dolls, fixing their hair, and playing in high-heeled shoes. I had my fair share of play with them, but not the same play I had with my boy cousins. I absolutely enjoyed my boy cousins more. I took on a "tomboy" persona that eventually grew into what felt like a real role in my life.

Baggy jeans, oversized t-shirts, timberland boots, and hats were my thing. And this was no reason to throw a red flag on the field and blow the whistle because back in the 90's- this is how many girls dressed. I felt masculine- yes, but did I feel gay? No!

Masculinity continued to make it known to me throughout high school. That same masculinity was packed in my luggage upon arrival to my college campus.

Exploration, space, and opportunity! I hadn't been on campus grounds for more than two weeks before my "tomboy" presentation caught the eye of an undeniably beautiful girl. Gay or straight, if you saw this girl in passing, your natural reaction would be, "Oh wow, she's beautiful."

I was in the study hall area when a letter from the same girl made its way down to my study area. From how it was given to me, I knew I needed to wait until I returned to my dorm room to read it. I had no idea that the letter sitting in my pocket was patiently waiting to be opened like a Pandora's box.

The moment I opened that letter and read it, the idea of homosexuality was introduced to me in a personal type of way. She liked me! The words danced across the page with charm as she inquired about my rhythm.

For the next few days, I spent time re-reading the letter, and quite honestly, I didn't know what to say. Days turned into restless nights, each one fueled with urgency to find the right answer.

If someone offered me shrimp, I would immediately say no, but thank you, I'm allergic. I wouldn't need a moment to figure out my answer. But in this case, my uncertainty hung in the air like a thick mist, overshadowing the clouds. I couldn't see my way to the answer, so instead, I went quiet.

Did my silence mean that I was possibly gay? Did the letter awaken feelings in me that were sitting dormant, and finally, space and opportunity presented itself? I needed answers.

I sat with myself until I could answer my "silence." The silence helped me come to a realization that I liked her. I watched the answer as it sat there in plain writing. However, I also felt something stirring from within that caused a conflict.

This feeling of conflict shook me enough to deny her advance, but with space and opportunity, homosexuality eventually entered my life in physical form. I couldn't contain my curiosity.

It was no longer this thought being contemplated over and over for days, nor was it just words being expressed on a sheet of paper. Pandora's box made its way to a different kind of sheet.

Our souls attached immediately. We became one on that college campus. Class was the only thing that robbed us of spending time together.

This girl gave me love that I had never experienced before. I'm not talking about the love that a mother provides to her child or the love that a sibling gives; this was different!

I wondered why, at eighteen years old, I couldn't imagine being with anyone else? What was causing this high level of magnetism?

Felt like our connection blossomed like a flower garden, nurturing and coddling me until I became seasoned. I became this well-seasoned homosexual on campus but undiscovered back at home. I hid it!

The hesitation to share the truth with my mom about my relationship should have been a cue that something was wrong, but I ignored that.

Let me add this before I go on. Anytime we have to hide something, it's a clear indication that it might not be in our best interest. This concept can be applied to all aspects of our lives: financially, socially, emotionally, spiritually, and mentally! When something is good, it's natural for humans to want to share it with everyone. However, when something is bad, we tend to hide it, and that's what I did. Nevertheless, it was inevitable that my mom and family would find out. My mom's reaction served as a testimony to depict how unpleased she was with my decision, but her opinion didn't stop me.

Months had gone by when the calls from my mom grew more frequent. She urged me to come home on a visit because she wanted to lay her eyes on me.

The moment I got there, her eyes examined me like a physician searching for something abnormal. I'm unsure what she may have envisioned in her mind before my arrival, but whatever she was looking for was not there. Maybe she thought I had run out and cut off body parts or even started some kind of hormonal pill. I was truly uncertain of her storyline.

"Mom, I'm the same Von who left here a few months ago."

I carried on in disbelief, "What did you think I did to my body?"

She had no words to explain. Tim/Tina was the only thing I could imagine that caused her interest to know what I now looked like. I grew up with a boy (well more like family) in my neighborhood who struggled with gender identity. This meant that he took on the features of a female. Clothing himself in female wear, putting makeup on his face, and jamming his size twelve feet into high heels, he stuffed his chest area with tissue paper and tucked his private parts to the back, making the bulge in his pants invisible.

Mom, "Did you think I would show up here with some type of beard?"

She was lost with more words to explain her urgency for my summons home. But after passing her physical check, I could see the relief etched across her face like a signature. And that's kind of where we left it.

My Uncle Den-Den also talked to me about the lifestyle I was living. At the time, he was a Deacon at his church and wore many hats in ministry. A law-abiding citizen, owned a landscaping business and a house, was raising a good family, and stayed on fire for God. People listened when he spoke!

While I didn't have all the details about Uncle Den-Den's life, I knew he was a changed man. He picked me up one summer day and carried me along with him to church. He didn't attack me with his words and wisdom or push his love for Jesus on me; he simply wanted me to know how awesome Jesus is! And he used himself as an example to show me how God changes things! You could see the "Christian" in him, too! Charismatic, likable, and inspiring. And he loved like a Christian, too. His inspiration encouraged me to believe I could finish college as long as I did my best.

During our drive to the church, I listened as he talked, but my mind was also preoccupied with the food he promised me, followed by random thoughts about my girl. Our night together was epic, and our conversation was heartfelt, but I was enthusiastic about exiting his truck and continuing my night to my liking. But again, I do believe that seeds were still being planted; I just didn't know!

Tupac Shakur wrote a poem, "The Rose That Grew from Concrete." The premise demonstrates how beauty and strength emerge from unlikely places. After reading that poem, I found myself in that rose. I was that unlikely place. The rose, a metaphor for my faith metastasizing within, its gentle petals unfolding, creating space for Holy Spirit. Only I didn't know it! Destiny was fighting on my behalf. Jesus was "proving nature's law to be wrong," proving that this world doesn't have the final say; rather, God does. This proves that what starts off as bad doesn't always end that way! He was growing me through these cracks, pushing me through unlikely conditions and circumstances. Only I didn't know it.

I spent two years with my college love before we came upon a fork in the road and decided to head in different directions. We had different goals and future endeavors, God knowing all about it. We just didn't know it. Breakups are known to be heart-wrenching, but for some reason, we simply drifted away like two sailboats riding the ocean on a peaceful night.

Go

The evidence of her heartbreak drizzled down her cheekbones before resting in the palms of her hands. The leftovers turned into thin crust and sat quietly in the corner of her eyelids.

It wasn't long before I met my second girlfriend. I looked up, and she was there. There to fill my time, my day, and the void I felt from being in a relationship with someone. The amount of time I spent with my new girlfriend doubled in years, plus some. I ended up being with her for five years.

There was a significant difference between my new girlfriend and my ex. She was older than me by six years;

I was twenty; she was twenty-six. Her personality compared to my "ex" contrasted day and night. Unlike my ex, my new girl lived life on the edge and exuded a certain dare about her. She was far away from a late-night cram session in some college dorm. She had a different course of study that surpassed dorm parties, basketball games, and college life.

It seemed like she had the world's weight resting comfortably on her shoulders. At least, that's what my whole twenty years of life perceived. And the dynamics in this relationship were different. It was so different that I grew up faster. While I was picking out courses for my next college semester, she was preparing to hit New York City in hopes of landing her next acting gig. She had connections to the music industry; if you looked closely enough, you could find her in a few music videos here and there.

I remember being on set with her for the Dennis Leary project. It was on this very set that she scored her first SAG credit. Some of her industry friends told her that enough of those credits would take her to the next level in acting. The thought of that pushed her even harder. It was like a battery that gave her more charge.

The need for her to do well and make money was dire.

We all need money and want to do well in life, but her need to "do well" hit differently. Her life depended on it. Life meaning her son! She had an eight-year-old boy whom she'd been away from for some time. On top of that, her mom passed away just a few years prior.

The first time she invited me over, I noticed the bible overlooking a shelf that was attached to her headboard. This bible had taken a beating. It was worn down, making it evident that someone had been using their frequent flyer miles to travel throughout that book.

"In a sarcastic manner, I said, "You read the bible?"

She answered me with an immediate yes. She referred to it as being her only help. The loss of her mother scarred her like a horrible tattoo artist. And the time spent away from her son was a constant beating that punched her strength weak.

Releasing the smoke from her lips in a skilled way, she continued on with her story. It seemed like I was quickly given the combination code to the place where her secret moments had been congregating. The stories went on like waterfalls. The evidence of her heartbreak drizzled down her cheekbones before resting in the palms of her hands. The leftovers turned into thin crust and sat quietly in the corner of her eyelids.

It was here that my empathy for people grew even stronger. Emotionally, I connected to her situation and cared deeply about her circumstances. I'm known to love people extremely hard. My mother's mother, grandma "Pie," was the same type of way; a very caring person. Her love for people stretched for miles.

Gram's church ministry took place in her home. She was unorthodox. Contrary to what was usual, traditional or accepted. You could find Grams on any given day at her sewing machine putting fabrics together, hemming someone's pants, or just threading needles. Her door was always open to the neighborhood, and her phone line seemed to belong to the entire community. When all else failed, everyone knew to call Gram's phone. And her love language manifested through her actions. She never turned anyone away. She simply loved on people.

My Uncle's friends would gather in the living room area on a Friday night while talking and drinking into the early hours of the next day. Upstairs, my older cousins and their friends gathered in a single room, warring to stay up to watch Showtime at the Apollo. Me? I could be found somewhere observing the scene quietly next to Gram's. Gram's never let me out of her sight as a kid. I had a front-row seat to what I thought was entertaining as a child. This was around 88-90'ish. It tickled me to see drunken adults dancing and singing in funny ways to the latest music waving from the stereo. During the course of the night, some of my uncle's friends would get stuck in position like they were playing freeze tag. And I could never understand how one could sleep right through all the chaos galloping between her walls.

Maturity, later down the road, let me know that this was no silly dance, no freeze tag, or no good night of sleep. It was a display of what addiction looked like. These addictions played like music to their ears, keeping them dancing all night long. Unfortunately, some of these men took their last breath to this very song. But Gram's never gave up on the afflicted. Her place felt somewhat like a refuge. Her empathy was unwavering.

I watched more smoke escape from her lips; some of it recaptured to be blown back out again. Words navigated through the weed smoke and made a statement into the air, "I gotta move from outta here,"

She'd been staying with a friend, and somehow, the expiration date surprised her like a gallon of milk.

I sat back, listening in disbelief. I mean, it wasn't the worst situation I've ever heard, but the back-to-back blows made me wonder if that's why her bible was so worn down. Was her faith the grounds for her to go forth? The woes in her life had run out of brake fluid as circumstances continued to drive down the busy highway. Yellow was unfamiliar, and Red simply didn't know her. Her circumstance didn't scare me, though.

She was like an unpolished piece of wood that needed sanding, varnish, and lacquer to acquire the high gloss hiding underneath. Somehow, I was thrown into her cutting, shaping, and sanding process. But aren't we all pieces of wood that need sanding, varnish, and lacquer to have a high gloss?

And I worked hard to help her through the process.

I was now a sophomore in college; I bounced like a ball between home and my college dorm. I was trying to balance my grades and still hang out with friends. I did all of this while still trying to adjust to the fact that I'm now living a homosexual lifestyle in front of everyone. My lifestyle was no longer tucked away at my previous school. My mom could lay her physical eyes on me and watch the movie.

Eventually, my girlfriend and I moved in together, which changed the dynamics of our relationship even more.

A bigger part of my life was now being sucked up by hers. Her problems overshadowed mine. And with each sucking, the larger my empathy for her grew. I learned a certain type of loyalty here. Yes, she was my partner, but more importantly, she was my friend, whom I couldn't imagine leaving out in the wilderness.

The circumstances didn't stop, but she always kept good faith in the Lord. She stood on high ground and never seemed to waver in believing God would help her. And although her relationship with God seemed twisted and diluted to me, I still listened when she talked about him.

There were some things I didn't seem to understand about Jesus, even in my twenties. So, I say diluted because she was the kind of believer who hot-boxed a blunt while thanking God for having a car. She had a very strange way of connecting with God. A bit unorthodox, but it highlighted God's promise to meet us where we are. And besides, I couldn't say much because at least she was talking to God. I wasn't.

We'd often ended our nights in great debates about God; these debates stuck out like sore thumbs, exhibiting my very own delusions about him.

I'd ask her things like why she always thanked God for paying our rent when it was us working our butts off. In return, she'd tell me that it's because of Jesus that we have jobs to even make money. And she didn't stop there. She'd talk about everything that God has done for us. Long talks like this usually rendered a night prayer as I found a comfortable position to rest in until morning.

Beams of light would awaken us the next morning as the radio powered itself on, turned to the same station, and played the same ole song.

Work, school, and hustle. Our days were hectic.

I was in over my head with this relationship sinking below sea level. I'm now 24 years old and finally about to graduate college. I wanted out, but I did not know how to walk away. How to end it! Did I even have a real reason? How could my feelings be justified? What happened to all the loyalty I had for her?

I found myself in that same quiet space, waiting for an answer. And the answer was simple, I wanted out because the weight of her world was too heavy for what I could hold. I felt like a weightlifter trying to deadlift barbells beyond the threshold. And it all began to slip from my hands.

She had to feel the slip. She had to feel the heartbeat in my chest radiating softer for her. If not for anything else, the lack of our bonding time should have sounded the alarm.

I'd lie in our bed pondering a way to break the news. Little did I know she already made her exit!

Lessons

"We know that all things work together for the good of those who love God."
—Romans 8:28

Nestled under the covers at my mom's house, I rested like a teenager in high school. I could hear my mom's footsteps growing closer to the spare room I was in. In a cheerful tone, she whispered, "I got food, have some?"

I could see the evidence of relief leaking everywhere as her demeanor gave a wave offering to Jesus, thanking him for the split. I dismissed the offense as I understood her position to protect her young cub.

While day and night merged, my heart worked on its mending. Despite my desire to leave my ex, I still missed her. I still longed to know how she was doing. Feelings of uneasiness still troubled my heart regarding her well-being. I still cared for her despite our rocky ending.

Our separation didn't end like my previous relationship. This breakup ended with no sail down the road while the violins spoke in harmony. We'd both hurt each other mutually. But there was still purpose in the relationship. Part of that purpose was God. I was a witness to what hope looked like up close and personal. I also learned what it meant to love God in a non-traditional way. She also inspired me to pray. I asked God to grant her every good thing that her heart desired.

Some are conditioned to believe that praying ought to be this long sermon to God, this perfect oration that sounds melodic. Not true. Prayer doesn't always sound like this fine-tuned utter that sings to the heavens like birds during the morning on a spring day. Simply talking to God with your heart brings him joy. And when you speak to God, don't just leave it there like a one-way conversation. Wait for him to speak back to you.

When we speak to someone in our natural life, we wait for the person we are communicating with to respond, right? The same rule applies and stands for when we're speaking to Jesus in spirit.

We have to wait for his response. But be careful here as receiving a response in our natural life looks different from how we receive a response in our spiritual life. This is where many of us lose communication with God. We miss the moment of response.

One may ask, well, how do you know when Jesus has responded? How do we know when God is talking to us? The first thing is this, pay attention and learn his voice. We must stick close to the word of God. C. S. Lewis, a well-known

Christian theologian, once said, "God's voice brings clarity'. So, in other words, nothing about his communication with us is contradictory. His message is always consistent with his character and aligns with his nature. If you feel you've heard a word from God, but the word goes against his nature, you must ask yourself, was that God? But don't give up! Pursue his voice and have an expectation that when you call out to him, he will answer. The next thing is this; refrain from putting a timeframe on when God should respond.

Continue in prayer and watch in the same with thanksgiving (**Col 4:2 KJV**).

Continue speaking to God until you feel peace and clarity about the matter. Don't always look for the answer to be a yes, as God does not always grant us what we want. When this happens, have faith and trust in him and know that he's making the right decisions on our behalf. Both yes and no answers are faith builders from God.

Again, God is always working on our behalf; even when we let the moment pass us by, he provides us a way of escape. Unfortunately, some of us go back knocking on the very door that God closed for us. And when we revisit the same sins, we invite more evil spirits to attach themselves to us, making the matter worse (**refer to Matthew, chapter 12**).

And this is exactly what happened to me. A few months after my breakup, I entered another relationship with a female. She was married.

I stayed with this woman for eight long years! So now we're talking about a two-year relationship, a five-year relationship, and now an eight-year relationship. We're talking about a woman who didn't have one child but had three.

None of this stopped me, though. My flesh longed to attach to the next woman. What she had to offer was enticing. Full of excitement and funny; we'd laugh until one of us had to call mercy. Sometimes, I had to hang up the phone because I couldn't take the stomach pains from all the laughter. She was all around a good person, just caught up in an unsettling marriage. I fell for her pretty quickly. And although a bunch of stolen moments summarized our relationship because she was married, she made me happy.

From the beginning, she told me that she wasn't going to hell over a woman. My follow-up question to her always referenced the other stuff she was doing.

Two weeks into our relationship she wrote me a letter explaining that we should end it before someone got hurt. As much as she wanted to exit the affair, our quick connection kept us in it.

Never once did I think about my contribution to their demise. The thrill of it all was seeing if she would really leave. The more she planned for a way of escape from her marriage, the more hopeful I became that she would solely be mine.

Her actions whispered promises, each gesture a gentle reminder that my position with her was solid. However, there were times I did question her true intentions to leave.

Holidays and visits to her in-laws reminded me that I was involved with someone living a double life. And the rock on her finger blinded me even more. Was she wearing the ring because she still had this deep-down everlasting hope for her marriage, or did she wear it simply because why not wear it?

Her struggle went on for years, and I allowed it. Eventually, her wedding ring found its way to her jewelry box to lay still with the rest of her unworn pieces collected throughout the years.

Gym bags with my clothing would take a rest in her bedroom. I took much pride in being able to leave my belongings at her house. My bags decorated the room like gold medals, proving the win.

We were together in the manner that we envisioned. We spent our days together without argument and frustration free of anything to complain about. Everything we had planned during our most intimate stolen moments now sat before us.

We'd lie down at night and wake up together in the morning, just as we had hoped for. Distance and time apart were now silenced. We'd talk dinner ideas during work hours and enjoy life with one another each evening.

We were known amongst the town as a couple as we'd go to the bars and clubs almost every weekend; it was routine. Even the bartenders knew about what time we'd be coming through. Her shot of tequila and my corona's sat ready on deck. My favorite bartender would throw his hands in the air each time, waving us over to our usual spot.

The guys in there had fake respect for me and mine; I knew they sat like savages waiting to holler at her. My ego boosted each time she'd pull me closer to her when a dude tried to shoot his shot. It was almost like a game.

The excitement of this relationship drove us closer and closer, but still, something kept her thoughts captured.

You could tell that whatever she felt could not be danced away at the club; even the drinks couldn't shake it.

Reality always showed up like a hangover the next day. At this time, I'm about a good twenty-nine, she thirty-five. She'd make our relationship feel as natural as it could, but the artificial flavoring still bled through to the truth each time. We'd spend our days in the house laughing and cracking on one another, dancing, watching movies, and doing what "natural relationships" do, but something about us always reminded her how unnatural we were.

I want to take a minute to pause and plug this right here.

The spirit of God will always give us discernment. When we act in a behavior that is against the will of God, our heart should feel conviction. Conviction is like an alarm that Holy Spirit sets off when sin is detected.

When it comes to sin, two things usually happen. Some people feel conviction, some people don't. The absence of conviction from God means that one's heart is hardened, causing a block for Holy Spirit to penetrate.

When this happens, it's easier to please our flesh. Sin feels natural. Although my girlfriend was in this relationship with me, her heart was not all the way hardened. One may ask, "How can your heart not be hardened if you are in sin?

It's called spiritual warfare. This is our flesh and spirit being at war. Her flesh squirmed, ready to satisfy the desires of this world, while her spirit fought feverously to put her flesh to death.

My heart was pretty much hardened because I didn't give much thought to it, and I enjoyed my relationships with women. My spirit did not feel the same warfare hers felt.

We'd go on for another year. It was the same routine between us, partying like rock stars all up and down the streets of Union County. Outwardly, the world looked like it was in our hands; inwardly, we were crashing. We'd break up just to find ourselves right back with one another.

At this time I'm about 30, she 36. It was on a random day that her thoughts about homosexuality breathed life. She ended our relationship abruptly. There was no warning; it just happened. We'd remained friends. I'd spend some nights with her, but eventually, our relationship faded. She'd go on to reconcile with her husband and birthed another child.

One of the last nights I spent with her, I had a dream, and Jesus spoke to me in this dream. In a soft, comforting tone, he whispered that he was coming up the stairs to enter the room I was sleeping in. He warned me not to be scared as he was about to knock on the door. In this dream, I could see my body rising into mid-air. It was like my spirit had lifted from my body while the remains of it were left asleep on the bed. A still peace existed in this dream, and once awake, that same peace lingered. Was that Jesus preparing me for what I was about to go through?

Saved

Being saved doesn't mean you're now pardoned from the desire of sin. It doesn't mean you'll never struggle with your flesh moving forward. It doesn't mean that you'll never sin again.

The events in my life began to blur together, unfolding quickly like scenes in a movie accelerating toward a dramatic climax. I'd experience a string of whirlwind romances that kept my life adventurous. But it was also during this period of time that I would experience frequent flashbacks to the dream I had at my ex's house. I spent a lot of time trying to figure out the significance of Jesus and why he came to visit me that night.

The more I thought about that dream, the more I felt movement in my spirit to go to church. I could feel a burning desire flaming from the inside.

I woke up one Sunday morning to find myself getting ready for church like I had the whole idea planned out the night before. The feeling about going to church sat comfortably in my heart, free of burden and weight. There was no tug of war. I didn't feel any inner conflict within. I was free from distraction as I headed over to my closet to find something to wear. Seemed like the perfect shirt and pants hung designated in the closet as if they were briefed about being worn to church.

My visits to church grew very much consistent. I even joined the church. One Sunday, I was in service when a mighty rush of power carried me to the altar. I stood before Pastor Bullock at Guiding Star Church and gave my life to Christ.

However, giving my life to Christ didn't stop my feelings of being attracted to women; it actually felt like the feeling only intensified.

And I think it's important for people to know that when you give your life to Christ, sometimes deliverance from sinful nature does not always manifest immediately. And getting saved doesn't pardon you from the desire to sin. It definitely doesn't mean that you'll never struggle with your flesh moving forward. And another thing, it doesn't mean that you will never sin again.

When you give your life to Christ, it means that you recognize Jesus as your only source of salvation. You're making an open declaration to live life for the Lord. It means that you believe that through Christ, you will gain the strength to overcome sinful nature.

After being saved, one typically finds a church and begins their journey of building a relationship with God through studying the bible. But this can vary as everyone's journey to Christ is unique. Many enter a period of sanctification. This is where we learn to die to our flesh daily. This is where we build self-control and learn to use the power of God to walk away from temptation. This didn't happen for me; well, at least I didn't think it was happening.

Thinking back to the day I got saved, I now realize that what I experienced in church was an emotional move. Not a spiritual move. Emotional moves are temporary. At that moment, it felt like the seeds planted in me had sprouted from their roots. I experienced tears in my eyes moving like sea waves as my spirit surfed the melodies from heaven. It felt like I was ready.

But my ride home served notice of the emotionalism that was perpetrated as something spiritual. I know so because after I got saved, I entertained three different women for the next two years before meeting my next girlfriend. We exchanged numbers but didn't connect as a couple until two years later. We met up on a summer night in mid-July in 2013 and have stayed connected since.

The age range between us was 14 years, but her maturity filled the huge age gap between us. Her charisma quickly captured not only my heart but the hearts of my family and friends, even my mother's. Her personality was bigger than most of the people I knew. She lived boldly; she was outspoken and fun. Strong-willed and daring, and it excited me. While my mother kept her beliefs about homosexuality, she still loved on her hard. Of all the women that had come into my life, I hadn't fallen for any of them the way I had fallen for her. She was different. She felt like a drug that I wanted more of each day. I couldn't get enough of her.

This is a great example of what I discussed in chapter three.

In chapter three, I mentioned that when God cleanses us of a sin, if we go back to revisit that same sin, more evil spirits will attach themselves to us upon re-entry, making the matter worse.

The spirit of attachment and stronghold entered here. I dove deeper into a lifestyle of homosexuality and experienced some of the wildest times of my life in this relationship. I mean everything that you could imagine happened in this relationship.

I recently read a book by Robyn Crawford titled, *"A Song for You."* If you don't know who Robyn is, she was the best friend of the late great Whitney Houston. Her book reminded me so much of my relationship with this girl.

Our relationship started off so innocently, just like theirs. The bond built between us meant so much more than homosexuality, just like the relationship between Robyn and Whitney. She was a friend! My person! My confidant! She was my personal support, and she backed me in every goal that ever crossed my mind. And I was the same thing back to her and more.

We'd travel together, flying high above the friendly skies. Jamaica, Miami, Virginia, D.C., Myrtle Beach, Philly, New York, Vegas, Maryland, Canada, just about every place in Jersey, and let me not forget countless times to AC. Life felt like bliss. Never a dull moment! Even on quiet nights, we'd find something to do.

Battle dancing in the middle of the floor and binge-watching movies often until the sun came up. Taking rides around town to feel the cool night air. We'd sit up on nights and just dream dreams.

For me, it wasn't long before our bond turned into those three words, "I love you!" My feelings betrayed me as we sat comfy in my room on one of those hot summer nights. How could I utter such deep words to someone so soon? The expression even shocked her as she told me I didn't know what I was talking about.

Sometimes, God places people in our lives for a certain reason, but we miss the purpose. We take the reason for certain unions out of context. Looking back, had I been able to discern correctly, I would have known she was sent to me for a different purpose, not a lover. All I knew was that when I looked into her eyes, I wanted to give her every piece of love that existed in me. She had a certain pull on me that tugged at my heart. Her mother had recently passed away, and I wanted her to know that she was still protected and loved. I felt a certain sense of immediate responsibility over her, and I made it a point to be that protective figure in her life.

And she was my crutch in certain areas as well, helping me to heal from past relationships and later walking along with me on my journey to Christ.

The irony of each woman I have ever been with is that they all came from Christian families and were invested in Christ. Her family owned a church just a few miles up the road from my church, so on Sundays, she'd head to her church, and I'd head to mine.

As our bond stitched us closer together, we'd blast off reminders that we weren't going to hell over a woman. I'm not sure if I really believed that statement or if I was just blasting off what my last girlfriend blasted off to me.

While strong bonds and attachments are built between men and women, a romantic relationship between women seems to create a different level of emotional bonding that intensifies the connection. Three weeks in a gay relationship basically equates to about two years in a heterosexual relationship, lol! This is how quick these types of bonds progress. Sounds like a stereotype, but it definitely has some truth to it. I've been there, so I know.

There's an old joke in the gay community created by Lea DeLaria. Lea Delaria is an openly gay American comedian, actress, and jazz singer.

Her joke goes like this:

"What does a Lesbian bring on a second date?" Answer: A U-Haul!

Hence, this means that women in same-sex relationships tend to fall in love and move in with one another really fast.

It's termed the "U-Haul Syndrome." Some suggest that U-Hauling in romantic relationships between women can be caused by an overproduction of oxytocin.

So, what exactly is oxytocin? Oxytocin takes on many responsibilities in our body neurologically, but it also serves as a hormone that releases the feeling of being in love. Some refer to it as the "love hormone." Can you imagine the intensity of two women releasing high levels of oxytocin at the same time? This could be why some women in same-sex relationships experience U-hauling.

Not to minimize the emotional connection that same-sex relationships feel, but sometimes these connections carry a neurologic reason as to why they tend to intensify so fast.

While there is a lot of science and biology behind human sexuality that we may not understand as a whole, we can look to Jesus for help to navigate such feelings that fall outside of his will for us. This applies to anything we struggle with that is not in alignment with the will of God.

> "Trust in the Lord with all your heart and lean not on your own understanding."
>
> —(Proverbs 3:5 NIV)

Here, God is letting us know that we will encounter some things that we simply won't understand, but with our trust in him, we will be led back to him.

The mind and the brain are very important parts of our body. It controls what we think and what we feel. Now, try adding Christianity to what we think and what we feel.

The factors sometimes collide leading us to feelings that don't always align with the word of God.

When this happens, your spirit and flesh are at war. The Bible tells us in the book of Galatians that the desires of the flesh are against the Spirit, and the desires of the Spirit are against the flesh. The two are at war, and if you know anything about war, there's usually just one winner.

Mommy

My mind was stuck in the moment trying to figure out how such a bad thing can happen to a beautiful person like my mother.

I traveled to the Pocono Resorts located in the state of Pennsylvania to spend the weekend with my partner. With the recent passing of her mother and the increased stress at work, a getaway was much needed. What better way to regroup and refocus other than to travel to the Pocono Mountains? Up there, the air was different. Each breath was taken in like that man from the Folgers coffee cup commercial. The birds hanging out in the trees chirped melodic sounds in their own tones. The mood was set on a very high frequency of relaxation.

Everything seemed to have moved in motion slowly, allowing us to regulate our minds, thoughts, and stress levels. The scenery was "country-like," offering the feeling of the Carolinas. The moment felt kind.

We'd returned to Jersey after a nice relaxing weekend of sipping wine, basking in spa treatments, and shopping. My mind underwent a reboot.

The ride back down summoned our famished stomachs to our favorite local Friendly's for a bite to eat. The mountains still played serenely in our minds when my phone's sudden ring shattered our laughter and moment of reminiscing. On the phone was my sister, calling to tell me that our mom was diagnosed with stage four cancer. She had known this information before we left for the mountains, but she didn't want to rob me of my getaway. The room fell silent as she delivered more details, leaving me stunned and speechless. The more she spoke, the more weight of the truth settled in. The room around me blurred, and for a moment, everything felt like it was slipping away. As her words continued to flow with such sadness, I grew angry and confused. The feeling of fear set in while a potent aroma of death passed by my nose. My eyes grew bigger as my throat began to close in on my airways.

I could hear my partner's voice in the background calmly saying, "Babe, what's wrong?" "Von!"

I heard her calling me, but I couldn't respond. I was stuck in the moment trying to figure out how such a bad thing can happen to a beautiful person like my mother. As I came to, I looked at my partner to relay the news. Our eyes stayed glued on one another as we both drowned in disbelief.

We hadn't noticed the waiter approaching our table.

"A burger and fries for you, my dear."

"Annnnnnd chicken fingers and fries for you."

The food looked appealing, but the news viciously spoiled our appetite. Our mood had gone from relaxed back to tense. Right back to the feeling I felt before heading into the mountains.

Oftentimes, when we hear bad news, we panic. We become emotional and unsure of what to do with the information received. The aftermath can be overwhelming, manifesting in different ways for each person. Emotional responses vary widely, from intense anger and deep sadness to feelings of isolation or desperation. Everyone copes differently. Some spend countless hours contacting family and friends to discuss the matter at hand. But let's not forget to pray. It changes things! There will be times of not knowing what to pray, but calling out the name of Jesus is sufficient.

Remember that he knows all our problems before they manifest in our lives. One may ask, well, if God knows every situation, why does he allow unfortunate things to occur?

We are not exempt from tribulation. God never promised us a life without pain and suffering. However, he does promise to wipe every tear from our eyes. He has the power to strengthen us and help us through each trying moment in our lives; we just have to believe in his power.

The next few days, I ghosted my mom for fear of facing her. It was inevitable that I would wake up one morning with the feeling in my heart to face the music. I prepared the words I would say to her and the words of encouragement I would give her. And I thought about the biggest hug I would greet her with.

I drove up to her house and turned the engine off as my mind continued to race in contemplation about going in. As I climbed the stone steps, the weight of my decision to see her sat heavily on my shoulders. She sat in the living room area as normal. The words I planned to say were held captive in my throat. My lips refused to part, and my voice grew mute. Instead of speaking, I did a surveillance of her body from afar in search of evidence from her stage four cancer. The silence between us hung like a fragile mist, waiting to be shattered with the first words. I knew she was hurting for me. Nonetheless, she put the bravest smile on her face and initiated our conversation.

"I'm making cabbage, have some?"

I sat at the table as the words eased out.

"Phiz told me what happened."

Without hesitation, she replied, "Yes, but that won't stop me; God is still good to me."

"I'm looking to the hills for a supernatural healing," she confidently claimed.

I sat in amazement as she walked through the house with a smile on her face. Knowing such bad news, how could she walk around with such uplifted spirits? She had this faith that was evident in her life. Unwavering! That type of faith was lacking in mine.

Over the next few months, my mom's life played out as normal. Physically, not much had changed with her. She stood a strong 5"6 in height, and she maintained her 170 pounds in weight. Her beautiful hair continued to flow down her shoulders, and the gap in her teeth remained exposed through her contagious smile.

Linda did what Linda usually does. The kitchen parties continued. She drove her car back and forth to the store fifty-nine- hundred times a day. She stayed committed to organizing the food giveaways in her food pantry at church. And surprisingly still watched my nieces and nephews.

The first physical change I noticed about my mom was the change in her voice. It had become very hoarse, eventually turning into a high-pitched light whisper. Once full-bodied and resonant, her words now emerged as fragile and delicate. But despite the change, she stayed in good spirits and never let up. She drove herself to chemo. She was relentless. She remained independent. Resilient- her faith was deeply rooted in Jesus.

The second change in my mom's body was her hair loss. Strands of her once luxuriant hair began to fall away. I had come in from work one day as she awaited my entry. I sat beside her on the bed, her eyes locked into mine, when her soft tone whispered, "Look!"

Reaching for her bandana, she revealed to me a completely bald head. Tears began en-route to my eyes as I pleaded with them to go back; I begged them to stop, as this was not the moment to show my mother that I was scared.

"I'm waiting for a supernatural healing," she called out, covering her head back up.

And although I agreed with her, I didn't understand what she fully meant by supernatural healing. All I could see was her body suffering physically. Her hair was gone, her voice had faded away, and she was losing massive weight from her body. At this point, her weight had probably fallen to about 130 pounds max. Whatever supernatural healing she awaited needed to hurry up and come.

About fifteen months into my mother's fight with cancer, the medication began to reject her body, and the cancer began to travel through her organs. The cancer moved in motion like NJ Transit. First stop, her throat; second stop, her hip; third stop, her stomach; and last stop, everywhere. The only thing that hadn't been affected was her spirit and faith in God.

The Warning

My mom was eager to get to church this one weekend; she told me she wanted to go there to talk about the hills. I made it a priority to do anything in my power to get her there. The next day approached with much quickness and anticipation. As I hopped out of the driver's seat and opened the back door, I smiled, ready to help mom take on her big day.

Only her slumped posture sat a world apart from what I expected. She was sitting in her chair on the porch, elbows pressed against her knees, lacking energy. The moment stole my Joy. I approached the chair where she was sitting, me still a committed cheerleader.

"You're a faithful servant of God," I uttered compassionately."

She lifted her head with great disappointment while staring at me in a moment that felt like forever. She managed to smile and take in short breaths of air. The unwanted tears were trying to revisit me again.

I encouraged her to go back upstairs to rest while still understanding the assignment. I knew I needed to go tell the pastor about what my mom had planned to do. My entry to the church doors at Healing and Deliverance replenished my joy.

"Glory be to God," the pastor shouted with authority.

She continued, "He will fight your battles."

Only moments later, the preacher spoke, "For I will look to the hills from where my help comes, my help comes from the Lorrrrrd!"

Those were the very words my mom was eager to get to church to speak about.

Nothing is a coincidence to God. He knows exactly what sits in our hearts. He is aware of the prayers we petition to the heavens. His grace is so kind that he sends us divine interventions to confirm that he hears us. Watch this! The Bible contains a total of 31,102 verses between the Old and New Testament, right! But the pastor preached the same scripture (Psalm 121) that my mother was eager to let everyone know about. One may look at it as happenstance, but I see it as God's perfection.

After church, I drove as fast as I could back to my mom's house, full of excitement about what had just happened at church. I wanted to let her know that the pastor preached about the hills. She looked at me with such gratification on her face as she pressed her head into the soft cotton pillow sitting nearby. The smile on her face called my tears back out; this time, I let them answer!

I turned around to exit the bedroom when I heard her calmly utter, "I've been supernaturally healed." A look into her eyes surprised me with a gift to see down into her soul. The answer I was looking for had revealed itself. I understood what her supernatural healing was, and she knew that I knew. But despite the revelation, I followed up with rhetorical questioning. "Mom, you're supernaturally healed?"

Her reply was peaceful as a dove, "Von, God did it. I'm supernaturally healed." She went on to explain that she felt no pain in her body. She repeated again that she was healed. Pulling the sheet back to examine her body, I pressed my hand against her neck, where the cancer sat nestled in.

"Do you feel that pain?" I asked.

"No pain, " she replied peacefully.

Carefully reaching down to her hip area, I asked,

"What about that? Do you feel that?"

"No pain", again she responded.

Mom's Birthday

Mom was hospitalized a few days short of Thanksgiving 2016. She desired to be home with us, but the doctor's words about her unstable condition left her disappointed. The cancer had overtaken her at this point.

Though she didn't come home, family visits, loving gestures from the hospital staff, and a special meal delivered to her brought the holiday to her room.

A few days after Thanksgiving, her doctor called my brother and I in for a meeting to discuss her condition even further. This time, hospice was the discussion. They wanted to place her in the left wing of the hospital and just wait for whatever came next. But with much fight and trust in God, she refused hospice in the hospital and requested to be sent home.

Day after day, she became more adamant about wanting to just go home. She placed us in the corner with her eye and demanded us to take her home at once. Whenever mom looked at us with a side eye, it was equivalent to her cracking a whip across our butts. We knew to follow her instructions and to follow them expeditiously. We had no other choice but to grant her wishes.

She was discharged from the hospital one week before her birthday. The EMTs delivered her home like a birthday gift. I could feel the cold air follow her into the living room, where she waited patiently for the EMT to loosen her from the straps on her stretcher. She was wrapped tightly in a bunch of white sheets like a baby. When the EMTs uncovered her face, she greeted us with a big ole Linda smile. Despite expecting her nurse to provide her with care, we were the designated caretakers for most of the day. The responsibility made me nervous as I cared so much for her well-being. Every cough and every slight movement kept me on high alert. We relied heavily on my sister as her calm and capable presence became our anchor. She'd pick mom's frail body up and transport her to the bathroom with no problem.

And when it came to eating, she was not afraid to feed her. Me, I was her entertainment. I danced for her, told corny jokes, played music for her, and talked to her about God. She told me to get rid of a few of my jokes because they weren't funny, lol!

The day had come, December 6, 2016. It was her birthday. We all gathered at her bedside, serenading her with Stevie Wonder's version of Happy Birthday. She rested so happily in her bed with a big smile. She eventually drifted off to sleep while we surrounded her. We sat there just looking at her and taking in the moment. Later that night, I thanked God for allowing my mother to see her 67th birthday.

The Nurse

The following day, the hospice nurse was assigned to come out and work with my mother. She spoke so highly about her in just one short shift with her. She called my mom kind, sweet and gentle. She even explained the peace that she feels when just sitting with her. I added on to complimenting my mother by sharing her life story and beautiful soul. I told her all about her generous spirit and impact on those who know her. I could have gone on for days.

The very next morning, I sat with my mom, and we sat comfortably talking to one another. She told me how beautiful I was and how great of a job everyone was doing with her care. She thanked me for helping her along the ride. She encouraged me to continue looking to the hills. In fact, she was firm about me never ceasing when looking to the hills! Whatever problems came, I needed to continue looking to the hills. As we spoke, the conversation began to feel like a farewell, filled with an unspoken understanding. And then she wished me well. I asked her if she was worried, she responded with a faithful no, but that wasn't how I felt; I was scared! But her gentle whisper to my soul let my thoughts rest in the supernatural healing she professed.

She requested that I go pick up her longtime partner, whom she had been with for fifteen years. He joined her by her bedside, playing the music the two once enjoyed. Luther Vandross' soft voice sang through the speaker as he picked her up to her feet, carrying her to the head of her hospital bed where the open floor stood. He slow-danced with her as tears painfully rolled down his cheeks. The spirit of thank you and completion was evident in the room.

The next morning, we all stood united in our roles as caretakers. The nurse came in, noticing immediately the change in mom's behavior. She advised that a backup nurse come out. Three long hours had passed before the doorbell finally rang. Her tardy arrival brought on a wave of mixed emotions, but her calm demeanor quickly steadied us for what was to come. We escorted the nurse upstairs to where my mom rested peacefully.

Within minutes of examining my mom, she called us out of the room, recommending that we discuss mom's condition elsewhere. She held no punches and told us the truth. She told us that my mom was actively dying. She explained that the moment was now here. Mom was about to transition. She instructed us to go find her end-of-life package. I had it stored in a safe and secure place in the back of her closet. I stared at the box, forcing my tears to stay back. I could feel them about to flow down my face, but they quickly receded as I thought about our farewell conversation. She was supernaturally healed, and she was looking to the hills.

I walked down the steps and placed the package gently on the table. Inside the box was the medication that would keep her calm and keep her out of pain. I didn't care about what was in the box, as I fully believed what my mom told me. She was supernaturally healed and not in pain. The nurse gave out instructions on what we needed to do.

My mother passed away about forty-five minutes after the nurse left. She was surrounded by family and friends. Before she passed, she opened her eyes just one more time. She couldn't smile with her lips, but her radiant smile was captured in her eyes. My sister and I stood over her with our arms interlocked, thanking and encouraging her to go home. We ensured her that her job here was done and that all would be ok amongst the family. Her very last breath seemed like the biggest gasp of air I've ever heard someone take. My Aunt

Diane called out for her, "Linda, Linda".

Just like that, she was set free.

Nostalgia

The death of my mother caused a shift in my life.

The final clearing out of my mom's house felt like a travel back into time where history and legacy replayed on the walls like a movie. The old photo albums she had collected over the years quickly became material of high value. Everything left behind felt cherish-worthy, even the salt shaker that sat lonely on the table. Her hands would never make their way back to season her favorite foods- but at least they didn't know so. Unlike me, I was missing her touch already. It felt like the objects in the room had it better than me. They didn't have to figure out life without her.

Climbing the stairs in agony, the movie continued as the tears in my eyes cried at the pictures hanging silently on the wall. Looking at my brother's portrait, I thought to myself, her firstborn son with whom she was very pleased. She was proud of us all. My nieces and nephews were next in order. My heart dropped a few more miles for them; how could they live life without Grandma?

The portraits carried me back to my school days. I was reminded of her hard work to ensure we had new clothes to flaunt as the new school year rolled in.

My heart wept in thanksgiving as I pondered the countless hours of overtime she cheerfully worked just to make ends meet. I thought about her selflessness. I began to apologize for complaining about the number of times we had to eat liver and onions for dinner or the times we had to go down to Grams house to eat chicken cacciatore.

The nostalgia went on. The feeling took me all the way back to the mid-eighties. It was around Christmas time. I saw a 13-inch black and white television sitting pretty inside a flyer from our local department store. I showed it to her with the hope that somehow it would end up under the Christmas tree.

I still remember the night she tried to discretely make her exit to fulfill my wishes. Tucked in my covers, conveniently faking my sleep, I headed for the window as soon as I heard her car door shut. The temperature outside was less than twenty degrees, and the amount of snow falling from the sky should have run her back in; instead, she carried on. Single parenthood did not stop her. And the weather was no competition against her determination. I fell deeper into thought. The feeling of gratitude overtook me.

The moment continued to climb with me until I finally reached the top of the staircase. Her room door stood opened before me as I peeked inside to glimpse at the empty bed. The room that once held my special person no longer felt the same. My body quickly discovered the true meaning of what numb felt like. I left there looking like a mirror image of how her house now felt, very much empty!

The death of my mother caused a shift in my life. As a people, we all handle death differently. Some people experience periods of depression, some people turn into bitter souls projecting their anger on others, and some become hopeless. Some flee the moment, escaping the reality of it all.

My mom's death hardened my heart a bit. To feel empathy became a challenge. I spent my whole life watching my family hand out empathy daily, but this new feeling of numbness stopped me from being able to produce it. No crisis compared to the loss of my mother. My new process was, so what- I bet you didn't lose your mother! Nobody's problem felt more tragic than the loss of her; I was withdrawn.

But how should we respond to death? You ever go to a funeral and everybody tells you, don't cry, it will be ok. Be strong! Or they might say you, oh so and so, in a better place now. These are all comforting words for the moment, but does that make everything ok? I've learned to embrace my emotions and cry when needed. Healing takes time. Bottling up your emotions will only lead you into a dangerous explosion later. Look to God for everything. Some may take that statement as cliché or dismiss it because they are not fully aware of his power, but I tell you this, it's a true statement! He is our healing virtue, protector, and prince of peace.

Death is not easy to accept, but it's more comforting when you know God and understand what eternal life is. When you understand that it's a divine order for God to come back for us. We should spend a lifetime preparing for the very moment.

We are only here on borrowed time to work for God. To prepare for his kingdom! Our works here reflect our readiness for eternal life. And when I say work, I'm not referring to how much money we sow into the church or how many church services we attend; I'm referring to our salvation and spreading of the gospel. Do not live this life thinking there's no life after death.

In the midst of storms, God helps us to win. When a person passes away, it's so easy for us to see it as a loss, but in reality- it's a birth and a victory. My mom didn't lose her battle against cancer. She won! She pressed, she stayed confident in the will of God, and she knew his presence was with her despite her circumstances. This is why she was able to smile during the darkest hours of her life.

Anxiety

The thought of death consumed me so much that it caused an onset of anxiety.

Many months of sorrow followed me after the death of my mom. My new days felt like limbo without her. I spent my time being stuck in time. The moments wouldn't relinquish. Moments like when my sister and I spent the whole day just sitting on her porch. My mind was stuck on hot days, cold beers, and good conversation while Cousin Hadi commanded the grill. Mom's making her way to the middle of the dance floor to show us the one-hand dance she'd been doing ever since I can remember.

We enjoyed aggravating her in a fun way, and as much as she clinched her mouth up at us to stop, we knew that she loved every bit of it. We did, too.

On nights, I'd sneak into her window to sleep on the couch, awaiting her footsteps to reach the bottom of the staircase the next morning. She'd wake up to a pleasant surprise that I was there. I could see her teeth piercing through her smile, even with my eyes closed shut. I knew this just by hearing the tone in the calling of my name. My heart yearned for just one more whisper. I'd pay anything to turn the clock back a few more times to feel the moment.

For days, I would sit in my apartment gazing out the window into the open sky, asking God to help me. Something was happening to me physically, emotionally, and mentally. Something in me was on full decline. I felt tired. I didn't have the strength to do much. I couldn't eat much, and my thoughts became fixated on death. I thought about what would happen to me if I were to die. Where would I go? Would I go to heaven? Would I go to hell? Or would I just be stuck in the ground along with nature?

The thought of death consumed me so much that it caused an onset of anxiety. One day, I was driving the highway when the feeling of panic closed in on me. I could not breathe. I could not swallow. My hands were shaking. Involuntarily, twitches jerked my body. My lips turned a certain hint of blue. I was desperate for air. My girlfriend grabbed the wheel and began to pray. We stopped completely on the highway as she began to call on God for help. As she assisted me from behind the wheel, my thoughts continued to run frantically in search of coordination between my brain and body so that I could move to the passenger seat. I wanted to move, but I couldn't.

The moment was silenced as I wept in the uncertainty of what was next. What happened next was a train of episodes just like the one I had on that highway.

I remember waking up one night fully convinced that I was about to die. I told my girlfriend to call the ambulance because it was about to happen. The same exact feeling came to revisit me again. I could not breathe. I could not swallow. My hands were shaking. Involuntarily, twitches jerked my body. My lips turned a certain hint of blue. I was desperate for air. Again, she began to pray while dialing 911 on the phone.

This went on for months. My girlfriend became so aware and in tune with my episodes that she would just pray before some of them started.

Anxiety had crippled me so bad to the point that I had to take an extended leave from work. I was experiencing attacks everywhere, in grocery stores, out in public, and even in restaurants. I couldn't even sit in the chair long enough to get my hair done by my stylist. I went weeks without my hair being done. And things seemed to only grow even worse for me. I couldn't drive my car or travel, and my appetite was depleted with each meal. I sipped things like soup just to get fluids into my body. I felt hopeless! At thirty-something years old, was this my new life?

I didn't want to be left alone. I depended on my girlfriend in a way that made me feel childlike, but-despite the big responsibility I put on her, she was there to calm me each time. Her prayers were always available.

I'd look in the mirror and see a person that once stood so strong, with such impact and influence, turn into this weak and vulnerable lost soul. Who was this person? And where did she come from? How did she get like this? And when was she going to get better?

The breaking point came on a day when the sun beat my girlfriend home. I knew so because I watched it rise into position. I experienced back-to-back attacks while she was gone.

I heard keys jingling in the doorway, followed by her entry. There I was, a grown woman timidly covered in tears, shaking in fear from being left alone. The bags under my eyes told her my story about what had happened for the last few hours.

Her frustration let loose throughout the house like an uncontrolled gun as she made demands on me like I was being held at gunpoint.

"Get up," she yelled!

Surprised at her response, I stood with full attention.

Tears softly rolled down my face! Room quiet!

She continued, "You can't live like this, and I can't see you live like this. There is nothing wrong with you. You're not going to die. We have been to the hospital ...you remember, right?"

Motioning my head to gesture yes, tears continued to flow.

"Monday morning, I'm taking you to Dr. Sharma because enough is enough. I'm telling your sister and brother what's happening because I can't do this alone."

I hadn't told anyone about what I was experiencing because I was ashamed and embarrassed. Moreover, I didn't want them to worry about me.

The next time I awoke, it was almost time for us to head out to see my doctor.

"Thomas, Chy-von-nee," my doctor called out with her thick, deep-rooted accent from India. My favorite patient, she referenced me. After reviewing my chart with memory, I noticed that the physical chart was sitting nearby just in case she needed backup. I'd been under the care of Dr. Sharma since a child; her family delivered me at JFK Hospital back in '78. She didn't need a chart to recall my history or to remember the names of my immediate family. On this day, she noticed a different demeanor about me.

What's wrong, why do you look like that? She grew immediately concerned for me as the symptoms I was having at home entered the room to show her. I could not breathe. I could not swallow. My hands were shaking. Involuntarily, twitches jerked my body. My lips turned a certain hint of blue.

I was desperate for air.

"Hun-nee, you have anxiety?"

That day, Dr. Sharma taught me a technique to help quiet my attacks. She also prescribed me a medication to assist with anxiety. I went a few days without taking the pills, but eventually, I surrendered to her recommendations.

Holding the bottle of pills in my hand right before bed, my girlfriend prayed for me. She prayed that the medication would help. She prayed that I would get back to life. She prayed that the medication was safe. I opened my mouth and let the pill fight down my throat.

I sat up, waiting for the drug to come take me down. I awoke around two in the morning feeling the effect of the medication. My body felt lethargic as I reached for my girlfriend.

"It shouldn't have to be this way," my talk was sluggish.

She touched my shoulder while guiding me back down to my pillow, telling me not to talk and to sleep.

Dream

Why would God take an interest in a sinner like me? How could my life be an asset to his will?

It only took a few weeks before I was back mentally strong. The attacks had come to a complete stop. I could sense my midnight blue 535xi BMW waiting to be tended to. I grabbed the key fob and hustled down the steps to take him out for a ride. The buttercream seats welcomed me in with a hug as I played with the features as if I had never driven him before.

Sunroof open with the music on high, I headed to the same highway that pushed me into captivity. Upon reaching the marker that first diagnosed me, I blew past it full throttle like a new cast member in the movie, fast and furious. I sat at the next light, thanking Jesus for all he's done for me. For bringing me through! For helping me in my time of need!

I began to talk to Jesus all the time. Anxiety humbled me. I now took nothing for granted. Every day, I woke up happy just because I was breathing normally. Everything I did, I told the Lord thank you. I made my first hair appointment. Thank you, Jesus. I was going out again; thank you, Jesus. I was back in the store's grocery shopping; thank you, Jesus. I returned to work; thank you, Jesus. I began thanking Jesus for the ordinary things I overlooked because I viewed them as just ordinary! These include things like having an appetite, being able to drive down the street with no issues, being able to spend time alone, and being able to walk the grocery store in freedom without fear. All these things were blessings from God!

The hand of God didn't stop there. He began speaking to me through dreams. In one specific dream, I watched myself walk down an aisle at a venue dressed in all white and with a microphone in my hand. He showed me a glimpse of myself spreading the gospel to people from all walks of life. This same dream visited me so often that I knew God was trying to tell me something? I just didn't know what.

Whatever he was revealing, I coined it as a mistake? Why would God take an interest in a sinner like me? How could my life be an asset to his will?

I ignored the dream for quite some time. To be frank, I was afraid to respond. Somehow, I knew that God would unlock something in me if I responded. I was aware that a birth would take place, and in that birth, a change would come about. I was thankful to God for bringing me through anxiety, but I didn't want him to change anything else about me. I was complacent with my life now. I was satisfied. I had my girlfriend and college degree, and my social life was right back where I wanted it to be.

Was God coming to break that up? The pursuit wouldn't let up. The next time I had the dream, it played out more vividly than ever. The colors in the room stood vibrant. I witnessed hues and complexions of colors I hadn't experienced before. This dream was different. When the dream came to an end, I sensed that his message was complete. This dream was the finale of the series of dreams I'd been watching in my sleep. In the dream, I knew his presence would leave if I didn't respond.

"What kind of plans do you have for me," I asked timidly.

I wanted him to tell me about his use for someone who loves women and lusted after the world.

His response was simple and unbothered.

"Come and see", he said.

"But I'm a mess," I reassured him.

None of this seemed to move him as he spoke again.

"I didn't ask you that," he gently whispered.

He went on, "I have work for you to do."

I would have been gone if I could have escaped this dream. Accept I couldn't wake myself up. I could only feel myself falling deeper into the dream until I gave God a willful answer.

"Ok, God, then show me!"

I committed myself to God in that dream. I awoke that morning fully aware of my encounter with him. Resting quietly in bed, I felt hesitation in my sitting up because I feared something would be different. However, I learned quickly that not too much had changed. My girlfriend was tucked in tight right next to me as the same flaws swam throughout me.

While attempting to wake her, the dream played in my thoughts, ready to explain how this time was different. This time, I wanted to seek out what he called me to do.

Her response exuded with happiness, but I wondered if she'd pondered what that meant for us.

We'd been on the fence about what direction we were going in regarding our relationship. We had recently made plans to go through with an IVF procedure for her to bear a child. We also had plans to marry and live a simple life like any other couple. Meanwhile, those close to us didn't even know we had those plans. And although we had these big plans set, we also often referenced what God thought about our plan. We knew the truth, but maybe we thought a new understanding would justify us.

World views change, God doesn't. The law of human nature will always have its own opinion.

But how do we determine what's right vs. what's wrong? That's an interesting question, right? C. S Lewis, a Christian theologian and author of "Mere Christianity," loosely put it like this: To argue what's right vs. wrong, one's view must be based upon some standard.

We all know the standard; it's innate, but sometimes circumstance, moral value, society, demographics, and one's upbringing can turn our innate thoughts ambiguous. We were actually born into ambiguity because of sin; however, through spiritual rebirth, our innate thoughts are restored.

Some of us get lost in transition. People like me. I struggled immensely; many days, I found myself suffocating in deep fogs of indecision. Stuck in what felt good to me. I spent hours combing through podcasts, looking for videos validating my feelings. And I found them. In fact, I found plenty of videos. People just like me, with circumstances just like me. Same-sex people attracted just like me and loved God just like me. I wasn't alone.

I had many questions for God. He gave an answer to each question. He often instructed me not to worry but to spend that time learning more about him. And that's what I did. I begin reading the bible in more depth. He showed me this scripture.

I held onto that scripture with a tight grip. It encouraged me to keep my eyes on him. Even when the snares of the "You will seek me and find me when you seek me with all your heart."
—(Jeremiah 29:13)

world came looking for me, desperate to place me back in the nest of deception, a place where I believed Jesus had no love for me.

That scripture encouraged me to believe that if I gave it my all, all is what I would receive in return from him. Flaws and all, I kept seeking. My heart was in it, but my faith was small.

But did you know that God only requires faith the size of a mustard seed? Mustard seeds are small in size; in fact, they were some of the smallest seeds during the time Jesus walked the earth. He used the smallest things to represent what little it takes to grow something big in size. If you know anything about mustard seeds, they grow into beautiful shrubs of all sizes. A mustard seed of faith is not to be excluded because, like a shrub, Jesus can grow it into a huge mountain of faith. That dream was my mustard seed.

Daddy

What was supposed to kill him actually gave him life.

It takes faith to believe what you can't see beyond the natural eye.

When you look in the mirror and see yourself gazing back at yourself, you see yourself externally. However, the mirror also has an infrared beam to show you what lives inside. But did you know that what you see in the mirror doesn't always reflect a true image of what's really there?

The most unattractive man or woman can look in the mirror and see nothing but beauty, while the prettiest girl alive sees nothing but a bunch of unattractiveness staring back at her. Does that make it true?

Phaedrus (fay-druhz), a famous Latin poet, once wrote a quote that goes, "Things are not always as they seem." Similar to what God told us right, "Walk by faith and not by sight?"

Unfortunately, we fall short in being quick to judge a book by its cover. A gay girl walking into a church sometimes gets viewed as a bunch of sin coming through the door, while a young dude clothed in red and covered with tattoos is thought of as a menace to society. A homeless man is seen as someone with less value, while a millionaire is considered a person with high prestige. But does that make it true?

Again, believing what you can't see beyond the natural eye takes faith.

I know exactly what God showed me through his series of dreams- however, my thoughts betrayed me each time I made contact with the mirror. I couldn't see the things God saw. I couldn't see beyond the natural eye. I saw someone still attracted to women who enjoyed dancing to the world's rhythm. And my focus remained on that. It's kind of hard to see change in the mirror when the inside of your skin still feels the same.

Even after God revealed his vision for me, doubt still appeared in my thoughts like unwanted visitors. They often stayed a long time asking me questions like, you really think your name gonna be in the book of life when it all ends, huh?

According to what some people said, I had too much world in me. I often felt the same way about myself, too.

How do you mute such thoughts? Where was the remote control to lower the volume? The power button would have been even better. This way, I could just turn it all off?

Where was I going wrong?

Where were my mustard seeds of faith?

And then God showed me something.

He showed me what he's done for other people. People like my father, who was healed from narcotics and alcoholism. Aunts and uncles, cousins and friends, all healed in the name of Jesus.

He showed me 1986. The weather was spring. The temperature in the car was stuffy. My shirt felt wet from being overworked at basketball practice. Who would've been the right person to remind Coach Gary that we were only eight years old? My sarcastic sense of humor, even as a kid, wanted to tell him, but what coach finds happiness in a rebellious player? Such talk guarantees one thing: a few more laps around the court. Coach Gary wasn't the one to be messed with. He showed us tough love. He even found time in his busy days to give us rides home.

Today was my day to hop a ride. Coach turned into my neighborhood as normal, but today, normal wasn't the posture. From the top of the hill, I saw my mother throwing clothes from the second floor of our apartment. Below the window was my father on a chase to catch every piece of clothing thrown from it. Hunched down in my seat, I hoped for Coach Gary to drive right by the chaos without recognizing the two causing it. And he did just that! I'd stayed at my Gram's house so much that he never knew where my actual apartment was. He drove off completely unaware that I was the offspring of the chaos.

That's the last time I remember dad living with us. The chain of events that would occur after that day had to be unintentional. I say 'unintentional' because what dad would intentionally skip out on spending time with his family? While I was too young to understand why his clothes were tossed from the window that day, I was old enough to feel the tunnel of love that bonded my father's heart to mine.

Days he'd sit up, telling jokes and dancing just to make me laugh. He loved doing this one dance called the "tighten up." I don't know which was funnier, the way he'd coordinate his feet together at once? Or the way he'd pull his pants up higher than George Jefferson! Either way, it was a sight to see.

And boom, just like that, he was out in the wilderness. The mid-nineteen eighties were cruel to some families, especially to those living amidst black communities. Street gambling took bill money, and crack cocaine swept from

Miami borders down into areas like L.A., Detroit, and New York City. New Jersey smuggled a good portion of the product, and "drug dealers" from Potter's Crossing knew where to get it.

My dad's hand was next in line to dab at it.

Death, masked in the form of rocks, came to take his life. I'm sure he didn't grasp the concept of family and friends crying over him as he lay still in a casket, but why not? That's because most of us can't see beyond the feeling that a thrill gives us. We often take things for granted. Some of us are arrogant or maybe even just naïve when it comes to mortality.

How often have you gone aboard wild goose rides and chases with the devil, fruitless pursuits? I recall drinking and operating a car without thinking of what could have happened until God showed me my redemption.

God did the same for my father. What was supposed to kill him actually gave him life. The video he sent me years later remains a remnant of God's promise to us.

His eyes glimmered life through his glasses as his new wife gave him the cue that the video had now started. He made sure his gold watch was on display to signify his well-doing. His time spent in the wilderness was untraceable. Tears of joy gathered together as he said, "Chyvonne, it's dad! As you can see, I'm in church real good. I could tell the moment was making him proud. He continued, "And I'm in the choir real good, too." His wit let me know that all was well. I could feel it. I could hear it. The joy in his voice gave me insight into some of his testimony. He had come full circle and was grateful for his new life in Christ. He was blessed with a do-over. He had two more children, a boy and a girl, with whom his fatherhood was redeemed. And although Dad passed just a few years after that video, I still knew that all was well. He died a believer in Christ!

In some cases, it's easier to embrace someone else's healing and deliverance because our physical body is not going through specific changes. I never got the chance to ask my dad what he experienced on his journey to Christ, but I'm sure it wasn't easy.

This is why I felt led to unpack my luggage. I want to help someone feel the experience. I want people to know that coming to Christ is a transformation that progresses over time. It's a slow walk that increases in speed. Knowledge and wisdom is the horsepower that controls our walk. Fuel (faith) is what grows our seeds. You can't drive a car without gas or it being charged, the same way you can't increase your walk in Christ without faith.

Oftentimes, we only see the end result. The finished product! The deliverance! The cleaned-up version! We don't have the liberty to capture the behind-the-scenes footage of everyone's life. Because of that, we sometimes become intimidated because we can't fathom how that person transformed. That's why testimony is important; it's vital (refer to 1 Thessalonians 5:11). It's a tool that provides encouragement to the next person and evidence that shows us God's power. His ability to transform.

Reminds me of some celebrities! We see the glitz and the glamour, the hit songs racing up billboard charts, but I often ponder what their life was like before the cameraman called, "Action"? Especially for celebrities who now walk with Christ. I wonder if their experience was anything like mine.

Money can buy anything in the world, but it cannot buy the moment of confession that Jesus is Lord. We must all come humbly, no matter our net worth.

The clock had just turned 8pm. The sunset colored the sky a beautiful burnt orange. The clouds within held a soft demeanor. The month was about late June. There was no need to rush out to the store; I had my six-pack of beer already at the table, keeping me company. My sticks of nicotine sat nearby. The vibe in the kitchen was set on acceptance. My thoughts danced like synchronized swimmers to one of my favorite songs, "Boo'd Up." On this night, Ella Mai expressed my feelings for me. Felt like she had me in mind when she entered the booth to lay the track down. My heart encountered each word as my emotions sang along with her to the open air: ♪♪♪ "Feelings, so deep in my feelings."

I couldn't help but think of her when the next part said, "I think I might die without you." Exactly what my mind was thinking. Recently, the person in the mirror said the same thing to me. Or maybe it was the cans of beer chiming in to share their viewpoint. My thoughts searched for a plan.

Like Peter in the boat out fishing (**refer to John 21:3**), my net came up empty. No plan, but I did gather up a bunch of memories from the years I put in.

Like that time, we went to South Beach, Miami. It was just the two of us out-running the city. Club LIV felt our presence. And then I thought about our trip to Canada. We almost missed the train because we stayed up all night arguing while at a friend's house. Some of our moments together felt like Bobby and Whitney; come morning, we turned into Mary and Meth singing, "You're all I need."

We had this connection that interlocked with my identity. The bond stretched past just loving her; and it was more than just this friendship. More than just this wild rollercoaster of fun spent together! Something deeper had manifested beyond what my natural eye could see.

The moment at the table grew sad as I reached forward to grab a stick of nicotine. I needed something to loosen up the tight grip on my thoughts that had been choking me all night. Although the music was still playing, the room grew awkwardly silent.

Another one of God's visions came to me. He showed me a glimpse of what I couldn't see. Like Peter, I cast my net back into the water, this time coming up with something.

A thought caught in the net said, "The first problem is your identity; you don't know who you are."

When you look in the mirror and see yourself gazing back at yourself, you see yourself externally, but get this; the mirror also has an infrared beam to show you what lives inside. But did you know that what you see in the mirror doesn't always reflect a true image of what's really there? I thought, well, who am I?

The moment had come in and left so fast that I would have missed the encounter if no seeds had ever been planted in me.

A teardrop fell upon the table as I put the music on pause. The sun had now set into the midnight sky, and the moon was now sitting at full attention. Eyes piercing through the bay window of my apartment, I counted the stars overlooking the universe. The moment was therapeutic.

God took me several months back. He showed me sitting in the same spot, gazing into the same sky, asking God for the same type of help.

The late hour helped me rest my head on the sofa. I managed to utter a few words into the atmosphere before surrendering my night to some well-needed rest. The last thing I remember before closing my eyes was asking God to show me who I was.

It takes faith to believe what you can't see beyond the natural eye. That night, God gave me more insight into what I couldn't see.

The Encounter

God operates in divine ways to allow for
certain moments to happen.

A seed of faith growing! The day was July 7, 2018. A Saturday! Not even two weeks later, I asked God to show me who I was. I had a lot of time on my hands to think to myself. I'd been staying close to the house, awaiting his revelation. Status with my girl was still in the state of touch and go, but for the most part, we were ok. We were co-existing! Our bond of friendship proved solid, but we still knew the inevitable.

To our circle of friends and family, I bet our relationship seemed somewhat toxic. Many times, I saw the same, but for me, what made the difference were the angles they couldn't see. Not many people knew how much we talked about God. And very few knew about our deep desire to have him in our lives. We desired him in a different capacity other than where we had actually placed him. We both understood the difference between acknowledging God and living a life according to his will.

There's a distinct difference between the two. One is to acknowledge His presence, authority, and power, and the other is to refrain from deliberate choices that block us from the will of his divine order. Again, my favorite saying was, "God knows my heart." That phrase is actually scripture (**refer to Luke 16:15**).

But what comes to mind when people say this? And furthermore, I wonder what people actually mean when they say it? For me, I used it in the context of letting Jesus know that I love him despite my deliberate wrongdoing at times. And I believe many others use this context for the same reason. But somewhere in my journey, God showed me the same context from a different viewpoint. He showed me how many call his name, but their hearts lie afar (**refer to Matthew 15:8**). I was tired of giving God lip service. I wanted to be more than a person who talked about my love for him; I wanted my actions and way of life to be reflective of him.

On this hot day, the weatherman reported the temperatures to be well invested into the 80's. This heat was the type that made a person unwilling to move during the day hours. I sat in the house, catching the cool air as I awaited the heat to break.

My phone vibrated on the couch; cousin Ty was calling to ask about the party. Hair undone, I couldn't see myself attending the occasion. Aunt Darlene's birthday was yesterday; today, she was celebrating fifty-nine years of life around the sun. The big bash was at her house. Seemed like her backyard sat on a few acres alone. The vision of the party was already in my head.

She had come a long way. I remember way back when she came to live with us. Word is that she shut down a few house parties my brother wasn't supposed to have while my mother was at work. At night, I'd sneak down the hall to take a peek at his friend's slow dance on the wall. Those days were long gone. Since then, she's claimed her forty acres and a mule. During the winter season, she'd text me pictures of the wildlife taking vacations in her backyard: deer, wild turkeys, foxes. I bet they all felt her love from afar.

The last time I'd been down to her house, I accompanied my mother. We sat all day in the open field underneath the canopy, talking about Jesus. Tranquility was the mood, a sense of peace and quiet. You could feel the presence of God resting.

Being around Aunt Darlene always gave me a sense of hope. Somehow, she always had insight into the bigger picture. You could hear the seeds of faith living in her just by the way she'd talk. There was no time to doubt or question Jesus when you were around her. She had a special way of ministering God's unconditional love for us. And she loved the family. She stood big on lifting us Thomas women up. For her to be the second youngest child in Grandma Lillie's tribe of thirteen, everyone listened when she spoke.

I shared with her my long stint away from the church, but she never was the one to judge. Because of that, I knew my conversations were always safe in her heart.

Now today, she was celebrating her birthday. Hair undone, scarf on my head, I knew I had to see her.

Arriving at her house that sat at the back corner of Somerset County, the cars lined the street high in number. I had my silver cans with me, and my partner was well fastened with her bottle of tipsy; you could feel a night to remember brewing in the air. My eyes found my aunt standing at the far end of her yard, enjoying family. I couldn't hurry my feet fast enough to embrace her with a hug. She had those kinds that made you want to hold on to her for just a little longer.

The family spread across the field like confetti; the moment made me proud. Up the hill was my brother tossing horseshoes with cousins while the aroma from the grill teased our stomachs. I made my rounds throughout the party before heading to the same spot where I last sat with my mother. Cozy underneath the canopy, I joined the family, talking about old times and reminiscing about family members who passed on.

I had no idea that a special moment was awaiting me and my girl just a few feet away. We'd encountered my cousin, a great Woman of God. The moment was already written. The hour. The day. Right there in the very spot we situated. No one really understood the spiritual warfare I'd been experiencing at home, but she did. She knew it without me having to tell her. She discerned it. Felt like God had sent her straight to us. She was his mouthpiece, his hands, and his feet. His love, his compassion, his encouragement, and his will.

She didn't judge us for having tipsy in our system; she was in our presence for one thing, and that was to share the love of God with us.

When we truly encounter Jesus, this is what we are supposed to feel. His love, his compassion, his encouragement, and his will. We're supposed to experience truth. She said some things that left us to ponder. A moment to reflect.

The conversation held me for the duration of the party. It was sobering. It overpowered my tipsy. It left me thinking about what happened two weeks ago when I asked God to show me who I was. Through our conversation, I got a glimpse of knowing myself. I was a child of God. Word by word, she divulged it. I know she had more to say, but she digressed. Have you ever had someone tell you, "That's all I will say for now?" The feeling was similar. Sometimes, we can't handle hearing everything at one time.

Before the night came to a happy closing, she extended an invitation for us to visit her church, where our cousin was the pastor. Pastor Staci Sawyer. We accepted the offer.

The ride home filled the car with a lot of "what if" scenarios. The first being "what if" we didn't go to the party. As I said before, some people believe in happenstance and moments of just because, but I knew it was fate and destiny that I was a part of this encounter. I knew it from the way it all unfolded.

God placed me at a party that I didn't plan to be at. He had me set my thoughts to the side about my appearance (hair being undone). He freed me from the worry of going to a party with a scarf on my head. And he stopped all forms of shallowness, which could have intervened with me being there.

How many times have we skipped out on going somewhere because our shape-up was overgrown, our hair looked like a bird's nest, or simply because we didn't have an outfit to wear? But God!

God operates in divine ways to allow for certain moments to happen. A missed turn on the highway doesn't always represent a mistake. Have you ever thought it to be God serving as a hedge of protection, from something harmful lurking just ahead? We like to say there's a reason for everything. I now refer to it as God being all-knowing. He knows things before we do. (Refer to Psalm 139:2).

I believe God placed me at my aunt's house to introduce me to New Life. A place where the setting was intimate, a place that offered the same compassion that Jesus does, and a place that understood my situation. From the way my cousin explained New Life to me, I knew this church was well-equipped to provide the spiritual support that I needed. A place that wouldn't pervert my vulnerability.

The next morning's sun beat us down through the window as we arose with much anticipation of what awaited us at New Life. Church music played loudly throughout the house, and the atmosphere was encouraging. The same feeling followed us to the car.

Through the front door, we entered the Sanctuary to find seating. The feeling I had while at home and during my car ride was still present. The smile on everyone's face greeted us with a loving welcome. I hadn't worshipped like this before. A house church. Pastor Sawyer built a sanctuary in the middle of her living room. Her husband was the organist and Elder, her son also an elder, her daughter the usher, and my other cousin, the evangelist. All family.

My eyes caught the attention of a big poster pinned up on the wall. I concentrated on the words that applied to me. According to the poster, I was in the right place. This church was like a hospital: a place for the lost, sick, addicted, and more. A reflection of God's promise from the book of Luke. "It is not the healthy who need a doctor, but the sick (Luke 5:31-32)."

The service exceeded more than what I anticipated. I experienced an intimate moment with God. The small gathering of people made it personal. And my cousin, Pastor Sawyer, delivered a word that spoke with such sound, clarity, compassion, and diligence. The experience was restorative. I left there with much courage. Hope. Gratitude and appreciation. It's always encouraging to hear someone tell you that God is working it out, but when you hear these words from a pastor, sometimes it resonates a little differently. It evokes a different feeling of security. By the end of the service, I knew my next return would be the following week.

I spent the next two years at New Life getting to know the word of God. Getting to know who Jesus is. The more I understood Jesus, the more I found my identity.

His Language

It's amazing how nicely we can decorate bad decisions!

2020 changed the lives of so many people. COVID-19 spread across the globe, claiming the lives of thousands of people.

Trump said the virus came from "Chi-na!"

Wherever it came from, no one was safe. Churches shut down, jobs shut down, and the unemployment rate was on the rise from state to state.

On this Tuesday morning, I walked through my sister's apartment, breathing in fresh ginger, orange peel, and cinnamon that steamed from the oversized pot. We often boiled this concoction to help keep the circulating air pure and fresh. We tried several remedies to stop the deadly virus from coming in. In my sister's house, the rules went: no one was coming in, and no one was going out. I was the exception to the rule. She allowed me to stay with her on a two-week stint while I awaited my move-in date at my new apartment. The days I did get out, "Sergeant Thomas" wanted details of my whereabouts before I could get back in.

COVID was that serious!

I found people's thoughts about COVID to be very colorful. Some had dark thoughts about it, while others colored the virus with light shades. I noticed the colors to be more eclectic amongst "church-folk". Depending on which folk you talked to, they'd tell you that COVID was the mark of the beast; it was a plague that God released upon the land, a test and a sign that we were in the last days; some would say, just pray. And some folk told me they weren't wearing masks because of their complete trust in God and that masks were unnecessary when covered by the blood of Jesus.

Of course, I believe that people who trust in God and have built authentic relationships with him are covered. But I also believe that God provides us with wise counsel. For example, if someone is supposed to take a certain medication or follow a certain regimen to remain healthy and safe, that doesn't take away from one's faith in God; consider it his provision sent to help you. I wore my mask with full faith and belief that he would heal the land.

Just pray made the most sense to me! I saw it as the common denominator in every circumstance that was rising. In the hospitals, we needed prayer. When a death occurred, we needed prayer. In the homes, we needed prayer. In the job force, we needed prayer. For our government, we needed prayer.

Prayer reconciles: It's a part of one's journey to Christ and a beautiful walk to experience. It opens our eyes to the many things that once blinded us. It gives us the strength to see circumstances from a different perspective because, in Christ, we are given a new vision.

COVID built my faith and prayer even more. In times of devastation, the light of God still beamed through the darkness that was happening all around me. I witnessed people come closer to God as a result of covid. People were praying more, people were depending on God more, people loved others more, and people still had hope.

My church family gathered every Tuesday for an hour of prayer via Zoom to intercede on behalf of those affected. On this day, I was the one in need of intercession.

Earlier that day, I had my weekly check-in with my supervisor, and the feedback wasn't positive. We'd been in disagreement about certain protocols and workflows that caused obvious tension between us. The tension grew so thick that the call ended with awkwardness.

I sat at the table in brokenness, pondering my efforts that had been unappreciated at work. The feeling of defeat was overwhelming. Thank God my hour of prayer was approaching fast. I dialed in and sat quietly on the phone while my thoughts ran wild like unleashed dogs. With each prayer and scripture shared, I could feel my worries being replaced with a certain magnitude of peace.

I could feel the presence of God in the room holding me together. His gift of tongue then fell upon me. Something I'd never experienced before. The utterance was involuntary. I could hear different languages pouring from my mouth. Sounds that I knew I couldn't form on my own. I heard languages that I couldn't translate. Though untranslatable, the sound was beautifully supernatural, somewhat melodic, and sweet sounding; it was an extraordinary feeling draped with an unexplainable force of calm. And, although I didn't know what was being said, I knew that my spirit and God were working well together in harmony. The two were in deep conversation. I stretched my arms open to signify my surrender to him. I wanted God to know that his holy language was welcome in my spirit.

I heard Pastor Sawyer say to me, "Just tell him yes!"

She became the interpreter of this divine encounter.

My cries then sang out yes, and boldly, the yes became louder.

My 'yes' came forth in my native tongue, English. I believe this happened to give me confirmation that I told God yes!

Yes, to whatever he had planned for me. Yes, that I trusted him. And yes, to believing his almighty power. He gave me the power to speak languages that I had never spoken before.

Speaking in the tongue is a gift from God. It's a form of communication that speaks directly to him. Holy Spirit takes control of your mouth and speaks mysteries with his spirit (**refer to 1st Corinthians 14:2**).

There are so many things that we can deny or doubt about God; however, when he shows us things in real-time, it's very hard to ignore the moment. If you have never spoken in tongue, I want you to imagine speaking a language that you have never ever spoken before.

Imagine one day you're praying in English, and then suddenly, your native language spiritually transforms into an unknown language.

Sounds a little scary, right? But speaking in tongue didn't quite scare me. It actually built me up. It gave me more evidence that the spirit of God was dwelling within.

My only job was to say yes to the birthing.

Later that day, I experienced nature differently. I didn't see the trees as just being full and leafy, but they had a certain smile about them. The sun wasn't just a ball of heat; I could see life in it. People walking down the street weren't just strangers anymore; I saw them as souls that God had blessed with another day to walk in his creation. I looked at things with more purpose. Like seeing little children play innocently on school grounds while teachers watched over their every move. This depiction now meant more than just recess time to me; it was a metaphor to remind me of how God watches over us as his children. Birds weren't just riding the sky aimlessly. They flew in still waters; no worries, a place of trust, even they knew that our heavenly Father would take care of their feeding. I could see scripture alive in the land.

God gave me a leash for the wild thoughts that were running through my mind like dogs. My yes soundproofed the noises that disturbed my peace. Like the birds, I began to soar in his still waters.

His strength is what pushed me to a place of casting my problems in his hands. This gave me more space to think about the good things.

I thought about my new apartment. The smell of the paint still lingered under my nose from time to time. I could still see the reflection of my structure through the wood floors from the day of the walk-through. I could envision myself sitting at my desk area, reading and building, creating and thinking about my yes.

I thought of those moments until they became the moment. The paperwork from the real estate company came back with a rejection, but God sent a family member to help see his plan through.

My feet ascended the staircase that led up to the door where my next chapter of intimate moments would reside. The dove-white paint gave an illusion to the length of the walls as I walked alongside them. Gently running my fingertips across the structure, the touch and texture were soothing. I sat in the middle of the floor in gratefulness while furnishing the place with only my eyes. The middle wall would take the place of my 55-inch TV. The sound system would be my choir on Sunday mornings. Songs like "He's Able" and "You're Amazing" would invite the spirit of God in. My desk would hug the L-shaped corner perfectly. On the wall in front of my desk, I could see my eyes hanging a huge abstract painting for the days I wanted to drift away in thought. Just around the short hallway, my California king would sit on top of a white shag rug to cover the remainder of the floor. I prayed for the room to remain authentic and pure. Empty of temptation and fleshy acts. Blackout curtains would keep the unwanted sun out on those bright and sunny days. Motivational wall art would tell a part of my story: Blessed, strong, kind, trusting, respectful, faithful, hopeful, honored, and loving. All gifts from Jesus.

Back in the living room, my oversized dream gray sectional would be my place to unwind. The bathroom would carry a beach house theme with mirrors along the walls where I could reflect. The rustic grey-brown table in the kitchen was already reserved for entertaining.

My eyes furnished a home that felt cozy and warm. The only thing that was undecided was the closet space. My girl and I had recently split, but circumstance placed us right back together down this quiet Union Street. She was moving back in as a "roommate." It's amazing how nicely we can decorate bad decisions!

Part of healing and strengthening in areas of vulnerability requires putting in a lot of work. You cannot expect to heal well from a relationship where the fire is continuously being fed. Breakups need time to build boundaries and create emotional stability. And although the split was mutual and our friendship was salvaged, we still needed time to align our emotional state of mind. Oftentimes, we underestimate the strength of emotional strongholds because, quite frankly, we focus on assassinating the physical part of the relationship.

God's instruction to refrain from physical (sexual) interaction with others before marriage wasn't said for nothing. There's more reason why he commands us to save ourselves. One of the reasons is that he doesn't want us to attach our souls to people who are not intended for us. Such sexual attachments can create a completely different path in our lives.

Did you know that emotional and sexual strongholds are spiritual? They are trapping mechanisms that can viscously attack our minds and thoughts. Unfortunately, thousands of people experience all kinds of strongholds without being aware that they are even in one. Especially when it comes to relationships! Fear of leaving relationships, co-dependency on people, having thoughts of thinking it's just easier to stay, asking yourself, well, who else would want me...these are all forms of emotional strongholds.

They have the ability to steal our identity. If we don't know who we are, then how can we function at our full potential? The only way to truly overcome these traps of imprisonment is to plant our feet in Christ. This is where the spiritual part comes in. Sounds so cliché right, but that's the answer in simplest form. A Christ-like mind overpowers anything that tries to keep us bound.

Furthermore, a mind like Christ gives us a new dimension of surety. Once we believe and fully understand that Jesus has come to free us, strongholds won't be able to keep their grip. It won't have anything to latch on to.

To a certain extent, I knew that my emotions were still bound because, some days, I invited the hold. Even after uttering my yes to Jesus. While I took a step closer to where he wanted me to be, a fear of embracing my true identity in him still lingered. I couldn't get past giving up "me." But God is so gracious that he works on us even when we don't see it or feel it. His impartation of healing is always active because he wants the best for us. Even when we make bad choices!

She chose the closet space built inside the bedroom. We both had clothes for days, but we managed to fit everything in comfortably. Union Street brought about a deeper connection with God in me and a clearer understanding of how to find my identity in Christ. It was here that I went further in living my life on purpose for Jesus. Reading more, studying more, and discovering my yes.

Part of my yes revealed itself a few weeks after my move to Union Street. I gathered my lunch and headed to my desk area to prepare myself for a session with my supervisor. The day felt typical. It was August 2020. A Friday, the 14th! Hot outside, and just about the same old routine happening at my desk: progress notes, calls to be made, claims to be followed up with, and an overload of tasks to be completed.

The Skype call came in, and the meeting began. The tone in my supervisor's voice gave me an indication that something was wrong, but I remained reserved. I sat calm in my seat and patiently awaited the regular. More disagreements and unsatisfactory comments about my workflow. But today, she got right down to the point.

"Chyvonne, today is your last day!"

My eyes widened as I tried to replay her words back in my head. I could feel my thoughts scrambling to put the sentence together. Only, I couldn't comprehend. Was I having an auditory hallucination? Or did she really just say, "Today is your last day!"

"It's just not working out," she went on.

To my surprise, I remained in a place of reserve. My thoughts had already left the meeting to go talk with God.

Was this a part of my yes?

God is all-knowing. He is aware of things before they actually manifest in our life. My moment of termination was no surprise to him but rather a revelation for me.

The moment was already discussed with God the day I communicated with him in tongue; I just didn't know it. He already made arrangements to heal me from the brokenness I felt at work. A plan of escape!

It's easy to trust God when we feel a sense of control over the matter. When the light at the end of the tunnel is visible. When our hand is partially gripping the matter. When favor is present. When things are going our way. But what about the times when we have lost control of the wheel? When the light at the end of the tunnel is somber? When our hand in it has lost its grip. When the opposition beat us like we stole something? When things are not going in the way that we desire?

Like losing a job!

I'd just moved into my apartment not even two months prior. We were at the height of COVID. The economy was in a rough position as inflation was on the rise. Employment opportunities seemed to be at a standstill. There couldn't have been a more inconvenient time for me to be terminated. And to nail the coffin shut, my supervisor hammered it with words of malice. I could feel her wanting to get full from my distress.

Her face carried a neutral expression, though I could see the laughter and celebration she carried on the inside. I could feel the moment being pleasurable for her. Especially when she hammered in the last nail; "And also, your insurance will lapse at 11:59pm tonight".

What do you call someone who enjoys someone else's pain or distress? A sadist! Contrary to the character of God. If only humanity could be a little bit more like Jesus. If only our compassion for people could stretch a little further. But blank stares held the presence of the

Skype call. Two minds at one meeting experiencing a moment with their own interpretation.

Symbolic to the poem written by Robert Frost in 1916.

I chose *"The Road Not Taken."* That made all the difference.

God's Plan

The urge to urinate awoke me from my sleep and summoned me to the bathroom. At the same time, the warmth of my California king awaited my quiet return. A quick transaction, except for God, had a different plan for me at this 3 o'clock hour. My feet dragged along the cooled floor to my desk area, where I sat tired. Curious to know, I obliged. Wiping the sleep away from my eyes, my hands searched for the power button to start my computer. The light from the screen illuminated the dark room as my fingers typed into the empty document, P.L.R! Parthenia. Linda. Richard. An acronym for my grandmother, mom, and uncle. God knows I've kept them packed in my heart from the first time I could feel emotion. Since their passing, I've given their names freedom to swim in my thoughts for as long as they could endure. But geesh, what a fine time for their names to take a swim. And then the big reveal happened. God showed me a vision of my own business; P.L.R was the given name. An organization to service young adults burdened with mental and behavioral health challenges. Workshops, life-skills building, transportation, and mentoring are destined to be its premise. An extension of what I have already been doing at work for the last 17 years.

There I sat at my desk, listening to his instruction whisper into my spirit. Obedience held me long enough to see the sunrise being welcomed into a brand new day. Released from the moment, I powered my computer off in appreciation of what just transpired. Another supernatural experience. The rest of his instruction took place in my dreams.

I walked away from my desk area with a plan, better yet, a gift from God that was delivered to me during the wee hours of the morning.

Have you ever found yourself awake at this time and stared at the wall, searching for answers to why you're even up? Your goal is to get back to sleep as soon as possible, but have you considered it to be God coming to spend time with you?

Did you know that the early hours of the morning, especially between 3am and 5am, are filled with deep spiritual encounters if you were to invite God in?

Here's why! I like the way Dr. Myles Munroe (a well-known Evangelist, Teacher, and Minister) explains it.

In a YouTube video published by Peek Motivation, Dr. Myles shares a revelation about the 3am hour:

He reveals to us that it's not a coincidence but rather a divine moment. A time when God is calling us to listen, reflect, and act. It's not just a sleep interruption. God speaks to us most clearly away from the distractions of the world. That time is between 3am and 5am. It's an intimate time when God wants to align us with his perfect plan for our lives. In these hours, our spirits are most receptive to the supernatural", Dr. Myles says.

So, in other words, we should not simply roll over and try to continue on in our sleep journey. But rather, take a moment to investigate why we are up.

According to Dr. Myles, this could be a time when God could be revealing something new to us: a new direction or a new opportunity. A new understanding of God's will for our life. Furthermore, it could be a vision that he has for us as it pertains to our future. So don't take the moment lightly. Allow this quiet time in. It could be a breakthrough and come with expectation as It's a divine invitation.

I could have ignored his instruction to sit at my desk, but his call emerged so deep in my spirit that I couldn't walk anywhere else, even if my feet wanted to. From this encounter, my divine moment with God, a business idea was birthed. And God gave it to me with specific instructions.

Moving when God tells us to move is essential in building a relationship with him. In order for us to grow in areas that we lack, we must follow his lead. Sometimes, we miss the moment because we drag our feet too slowly. We don't trust where the spirit of God is leading us to go. Sometimes, we doubt his instruction. And as a result, the opportunity passes us by. It's almost like calling for help and then refusing assistance when the help arrives.

God heard my cry for help. He knew how bothersome the job had become for me. I just needed to be ready when his help arrived. I had to be ready to embrace and trust him no matter what the plan looked like. Now, amid God's elevation and preparation for us to go in a different direction, sometimes we may encounter unfortunate circumstances for some time. But don't let this serve as discouragement. It's not a setback; it's a setup!

I had to be terminated in order to be where I am today. In order to work in the capacity that was best fitting for me, I had to let go of a traditional way of working. God prepared me with a business mindset to generate income in an unorthodox type of way. But I had to move when he said move. I had to put all of my trust in him and go!

Since coming to Christ, I've learned the importance of time and the importance of using the bible as a guidebook to understand how history paves the way for my future. Many people bypass the reading of scripture and sometimes become bored with it because the stories are viewed as being outdated to the times that we live in today. Yes, indeed, some stories date back to ancient times, but these stories are still progressive. This means that what you read in the bible can still be applied to your life today. God is still helping his people today from a context that was recorded over 2,000 years ago. When God called me to my desk, I considered it an Abraham moment.

God called Abraham to travel to another place where a blessing awaited him. He had no idea where this place was. However, he went because he trusted God. Because of his obedience to follow the instruction of God, Abraham received an inheritance beyond his imagination (refer to Genesis chapter 12-22).

I challenge you to let God navigate your next move!

In the Water

*On the outside, I smiled, but on the inside,
my soul experienced its very own castaway.*

August 8th, 2021 marked a special day in my life. My church hosted a family and friend's day, something held annually, but this year coined a different meaning for me. Today, I was being baptized. I could see the Elder of the church preparing the pool from afar as Pastor Sawyer anointed the water in prayer. I sat alone in the changing area, yearning for the presence of my mother. I caught a vision of her smile, and that made me smile. Just the mere thought of her sufficed. Made me grateful. Made me thankful for each seed she planted in me when I was young. In her absence stood my sister and brother. My nieces and nephews. Cousins and friends. Old and young gathered around to witness a soul make a public declaration to be a follower of Jesus Christ.

The ceremony didn't take place in this big sanctuary where church decorations and a big choir struck a chord of emotionalism in me. Everything I felt was pure. There, I sat in the middle of a park tucked away on the south side of Edison, and that was more than good.

Gazing down the hill onto the open field, I saw children run effortlessly through the green pastures. Oblivious to the sacred moment that sat just ahead, their energy kept the swings and sliding boards overworked.

Reminded me of my childhood days when my friends and I ran about the wooden jungle gym in the old park. We'd spend hours on the swing practicing how to make a perfect landing after jumping from it mid-air. To quench our thirst, we'd knock on Ms. Edy's door to collect our favorite popsicles. She molded them from used pop sticks we found in the neighborhood earlier that day.

My mind became quickly distracted.

I could taste the germs still dancing around my mouth from over thirty years ago. But like the innocent children that ran about the green pastures, we didn't know any better. But they weren't the only ones to wear badges of innocence in the field. I also saw a few adults dripping milk from their inner man as well. They, too, were oblivious to the sacred moment that sat just ahead.

The call to gather rang out like a school bell. The moment arrived. I sat in the water, anticipating my body to be immersed. I could feel my brother overlooking the pool from just a few feet shy from me. And then it happened.

"Sister Von, I baptize you in the name of the Father, and of the Son, and of the Holy Spirit." Those were the last words I heard before my whole body was submerged underwater.

When someone gets baptized, it serves as a symbol of purification and a rebirthing into a new life in Christ. The water does not hold special powers to block you from sin; rather, it's more of a testament to your faith that Jesus' death on the cross paid for our sins. The water is a metaphor to depict cleanliness. It represents the character of Christ. When you step into the water, you are stepping into Christ, and when you emerge from it, you are drenched with his spirit. A renewing happens. Your spirit resets. You become a new creature.

And there I stood with my thumb on the page, ready to read something new in my life. Back at my seat, I wondered what God had for me next.

I bet the minds of the oblivion already pictured my life to move like those synchronized swimmers. In hindsight, their depiction was partially right. On the outside, I smiled, but on the inside, my soul experienced its very own castaway.

I was Tom Hank's character "Chuck" thrown into the sea trying to survive. Daily challenges of life stood tall like big kahuna waves crashing down on me.

One came in only a few months after my baptism, and the wave capsized me. It happened on a Tuesday night right before bible study. I received a message from my pastor to join in on a Zoom call. She shared some news with me that drowned my spirit. While underwater, the moment motioned back in time to the day my sister told me that our mom had cancer. And now, pastor.

She sat beside her husband and uttered the words with such resolve. Her faith in Christ is what kept her strengthened. I wanted to have that same strength, but I didn't. Too many waves were crashing down on me all at once. I was still trying to get my breath back from the loss of my Aunt Darlene's untimely death. This news threw me back into the trenches. Questioning and wondering, why God? I needed an exit.

But like "Chuck," there was no overnight rescue. He spent a thousand days alone in the wilderness trying to find his way back to humanity; mine were spent digging and planting my feet deeper in Christ, trying to find the strength I needed.

The waves continued to build. The next one that rushed in was a complete wipeout. I didn't have time to stabilize my feet.

Her belongings lined the walls, ready to be carried out to her new place of stay. The closet door stood open, empty and alone. We'd had a disagreement, but my calculations didn't add it up to equal a move-out!

A bad time for her to leave was the thoughts I had in mind. I was emotionally fragile. My pastor was sick. I was still trying to build my business. Life felt hectic.

I sat alone one night and allowed my emotions to express each feeling that was beating in my heart.

My cries asked God to relieve me from what I was feeling inside: defeated, scared, and alone. How does one overcome?

As humans, we all experience "cast away" moments. Moments when we feel as though our life has shipwrecked or crashed. Moments of feeling like we have lost it all. Moments of feeling separated from society. These moments feel like waves washed ashore, drowning us out from our visions and dreams, goals and aspirations.

But the question is, how do you handle your castaway moment? How do you handle your "Chuck?"

In the movie Cast Away, "Chuck" found a soccer ball and named it Wilson! Desperate for any glimpse of socialization, he drew a face on it and talked to the ball as if it were a human.

Later on in the movie, he recouped a FedEx box that was stamped with angel wings. A spiritual encounter that gave him hope.

I found my angel wings in a word decal that had been staring at me the whole time. The decal on the wall said, Faith! The substance of things hoped for, the evidence of things not seen.

Kind of like when a bill is due, and you have no idea where the funds will come from. Somewhere in your heart, you trust that the funds will appear right on time. That's faith! Or when a doctor gives you a prognosis about a family member that's not favorable. Somewhere in your heart, you believe that no matter what, all will be ok. That's faith! Believing in Jesus, that's faith!

Faith was the only leg I had to stand on. I kept my mind focused on the promises that God showed me. I woke up one morning and noticed my pillow to be free of wetness from the tears. Inside, I smiled. Peace was with me.

I survived the storm just like "Chuck." I was him floating on a raft in the middle of the sea at Noonday. A big ship came by, blowing the horn to signify my rescue.

Back on land, "Chuck's cast away moment blessed him with a new interpretation of life. The movie comes to an end where he finds himself standing in an intersection, a crossroad. He's left with a decision to pursue the old or move forward with the new.

After my baptism, I found myself standing in that same spot. Like "Chuck" I was faced with the same decision. Pursue the old or move forward with the new. I chose the road that led to the new. I handled my Chuck with faith!

The Purge

Have you ever experienced a time in your life when you've made up your mind to do a certain thing? Like saving up a certain amount of money, or maybe you've decided to return back to school. Maybe you've made a vow to lose a certain amount of weight. You've made a public announcement to your family and friends. You posted something on social media to let everyone know about the new journey that you're on. You wrote it down in your journal. You created a plan of action. You can see the vision as clear as day.

The excitement that you feel on the inside overwhelms you to the point of overjoy. And then suddenly, something happens to distract you from your vision. The money you've been laying aside for that certain thing now has to be spent on an unexpected bill that can't be put off. Your journey to losing weight seems sabotaged by the five invites you received to attend dinner parties. The school that you've had your eye on has now increased its tuition by thirty percent. The feeling of overjoy and excitement starts to lose its steam. Your vision now turns into a virtual tombstone: silent and without life! You find yourself left with the memories of what you were going to do.

Your old ways of thinking begin to creep and shimmy their way into the new mindset that you made a solid decision to have. You find yourself back at square one. The cup is now looking empty!

Have you ever wondered why these types of things happen? I know I have! I've always referred to them as "just because" moments.

I now understand that these "just because" moments aren't "just because."

What I'm about to say may resonate a little deep for those who don't understand or recognize conflict on a spiritual level. The answer is this, satan is real. He is a destructive force that comes to kill, steal, and destroy. Just like the bible tells us in the book of John. Satan hates to see God's children win. He will do anything to distract us from the journey and relationship that we have with God. He will go beyond all measures to create space for doubt to play in our minds about the power of God and the rule that God has over our lives. He attempts to bring us down through the use of strongholds, emotional soul ties, and familiarity. He is aware of our weak points and struggle areas. His number one goal is to dangle temptation over our heads so that we will participate in acts that do not align with the word of God.

The moment a drug-addicted individual makes a vow to cleanse their soul of drugs, a pusher comes along to offer up a free hit. That woman that takes a stand to walk away from prostitution is reeled back into the industry with large amounts of money from her pimp.

These are not "just because" moments. These are well-put-together tactics from the trick of the enemy to keep one bound.

Satan moves like a snake, slick and sly; in some instances, we miss his entry point. Especially when he enters from familiar places! Places like close friends, loved ones, and environments where we have let our inhibitors down: Places where we have allowed ourselves to be vulnerable.

Now let me ask you this, have you ever experienced opposition or even betrayal from a close friend or maybe a family member? Could it be a co-worker? How did you respond? Not all, but most of us respond with anger and bitterness. We want to get even; in some cases, we find ourselves acting out of character.

We look at the situation or circumstance from a surface-level standpoint, bypassing what actually lies at the root. Our actions become the by-product of what satan strategically put together behind the scenes.

It's our natural instinct to respond when we feel under attack from someone or something. Our adrenaline activates, and the feeling of fight-or-flight moves into action.

We want to protect ourselves. However, in some cases, we allow our egos to play a part, and it is right here where satan attempts to make his entry. He wants us to respond in a flesh-type manner, meaning the way of the world, to discredit the God that abides in us. And it only takes a split second for our flesh to respond destructively. After the moment has passed, many of us have even said to ourselves, "I don't know what got into me?"

I found myself saying this on July 3, 2023. The hour was about eleven o'clock. The night air rested humid and still. The events of the afternoon had sucked me so emotionally dry that sleep was the only prayer I sent up to God. My mind was exhausted. I had not one more tear in me to cry. In fact, I'd been crying so much throughout the day that laughter was the only thing left in me to do.

I fell down on my couch and powered the TV on. I went on a search to find the name of that song written by Greg O'Quin, "I Told the Storm."

Even though your winds blow
I want you to know:
You cause me no alarm,
Cause I'm safe in his arms.
Even though your rain falls,
I can still make this call:
Let there be peace.
Now I can say, "Go away!"
I command you to move today.
Because of faith, I have a brand new day.
The sun will shine – and I will be okay.
That's when I told the storm!
I told the storm to pass.
Storm, you can't last!
Go away – I command you to move today.
Storm - when God speaks...
Storm - you've got to cease!
That's what I told storm!
Wind – stop blowing!
Flood – stop flowing!
Lightning – stop flashing!
Breakers – stop dashing!
Darkness – go away!
Clouds – move away!
That's what I told the storm!
Death can't shake me!
Job can't make me!
Bills can't break me!
You can't drown me –

Cause my Gods surrounds me!
That's what I told the storm!

The power of the song picked me up to my feet as I thanked God for the reminder. And then I heard a knock at the door. From the door viewer, I saw the person who had been causing my tears standing in my hallway. Vulnerable, I gave way for entry. I noticed she wasn't alone. With her stood the other person responsible for the cause of my pain from the early day. The same face I had loved on since 2013. A heated discussion ensued. My thoughts began to lose control.

That night, opposition attempted to **kill** my identity in Christ, **steal** the progression over my life, and **destroy** the plans that God had for me.

A split second of making a violent decision landed me in the hospital that night. And, as I sat in the hospital bed while doctors tended to me, God brought back to my remembrance the song I had been playing all night: "I told the storm."

My brother sat along my bedside. His demeanor was calm, but his instruction was stern. We'd revisit the many lessons he's taught me over the years, which carried me to the same place of his mind space. Calm!

The next morning, I left the hospital in a brace to cover the sutures that had been placed in five different parts of my hand. Discharge instructions to follow up with an orthopedic surgeon to repair the torn tendon in my middle finger. To this day, I have no feeling in my ring finger. All because of a bad decision!

Redeemed, satan wasn't satisfied. One week later, I'd end up in the same hospital with a staph infection from my wounds. IVs and fluids ran through my body to cleanse the bacteria from infiltrating my bloodstream. I spent four days of stillness in a hospital bed with plenty of quiet time to talk with God.

My bible rested beside me as I parted my lips to speak.

"God, why is this happening to me?"

I looked around the room in despair as I awaited his gentle response.

He said, "*This has nothing to do with you. In fact, this has nothing to do with your offenders.*"

My soul craved more answers as the spirit of God continued to feed me.

He went on, "*Distraction was the plan of the enemy, and the familiar faces were just pawns.*"

But why? Like an unsatisfied child, I asked again.

And he answered, "*Because of the God that is in you-forgive my daughter, forgive!*"

God went silent in the room to give me space to reflect, meditate, and think about his feeding. And as I ate, I could taste his purge. It awoke the pallet on my tongue like a fine seasoning. Bold and strong like fresh garlic, the remnants stuck with me all day long.

I understood the assignment.

It was time to allow the door to shut. I had been holding on to people, places, and things that were causing distraction. Bounding me like quicksand, but God's promises reached down to pull me back up. That's the awesome thing about God! He is more powerful than any force of evil.

Just when satan makes us feel like he's winning, God shows up to display who has the ultimate power, even during our own sabotage.

He comes to close those doors that are too weighty for us to shut alone. And this is where the purge happens.

The purge can manifest as many things: losing friends, leaving a relationship, backing away from certain circles, taking on a different position at work, halting substance abuse, etc.

The grace of God showed me those areas where my pruning and purging would take place. He helped me identify the people, the places, and the things that were tied to my strongholds. I just needed enough faith in

Jesus to believe that he would lead me through the storm.

My purge loosely reminds me of the story of Joseph from the bible in the book of Genesis. He was the second youngest brother of twelve siblings who was gifted with dreams and visions sent by God. His divine ability set him apart from his brothers, making him special in the eyes of his biological father. When Joseph shared his abilities with his brothers, they didn't receive the news well. They grew jealous of Joseph and ultimately came up with a plot to get rid of him. How could a group of brothers commit such betrayal against their own sibling? Did they hate Joseph that much? I would say no, they didn't; they just hated the authority that God gave him and the plans for his life.

Satan used his brothers as pawns to offset Joseph from the path that God had him on. Joseph was thrown in a pit by his brothers and later sold to a group of Arabs who brought him into Egypt. But God was with Joseph and prospered him. He'd go on to interpret dreams and visions throughout the land of Egypt. Even in his new place of stay, Joseph faced opposition, but God was with him. He was thrown in prison after being slandered, but still, God was with him. Even in prison, the favor of God fell upon Joseph.

Joseph spent three years in prison, and while there, he continued his ministry of prophecy and interpreting dreams until the day of his release.

He'd return back to Egypt as an overseer of the crops, where he would encounter his brothers. The same ones that threw him in the pit and attempted to get rid of him.

But Joseph didn't retaliate- he forgave and blessed his family with crops. He told his brothers, "Fear not: I am in a place of God. He let his brothers know that what the enemy meant for bad, God made it for good. While my siblings weren't the people who betrayed me, the story of Joseph helped me to better understand how to handle betrayal and how to forgive. Furthermore, how to hold on to God's vision and how to weather the storm.

The storm is our purging period: a time of maturing in God and learning how to use the Spirit of God to overcome situations. It's a time of gaining wisdom and discernment to live out the will of God. Purging is necessary when pursuing God. It's a requirement. It's a part of how we cleanse our souls. There has to be a cutting off of certain things. Satan tries to pervert our period of purging with distractions because he wants to keep us bound. He wants us to have doubt in God when we struggle in a storm or through a time of pruning and purging.

I endured a lot of emotional pain during my period of purging, and finding my identity in Christ. But, when the rain cleared just as God promised, my vision became clear.

What looked like a trap was really my Exodus (exit). And what looked like a loss was really a victory.

Evangelism

I found myself rummaging through old letters that my pastor and I had exchanged, the words still holding a deep significance.

Often, she'd read my letters during her chemotherapy or radiation sessions to help transition her into a place of solace. For nearly two years, God had me write her every week, consistently and faithfully. Words of encouragement stood in line to overcrowd the pages while my witty jokes put her in position for a good laugh. During this time, I'd also give her updates about my continued walk in Christ, keeping her abreast of my travel.

If I were to describe our letters of exchange, I'd tell you that they tasted like a good bowl of chicken noodle soup for the soul – Quite therapeutic, bond-building, and spiritually connecting. They were God's divine preparation and instruction for a time that was soon to come.

Oftentimes, we overlook the needs of a pastor because we assume that pastors have it all together. We think that because they are in leadership and are set aside to feed the word of God to their flock, they don't need to be fed as well. I found it an honor that God entrusted me to supply my pastor with messages to uplift her spirit. And I know for sure that these letters served as good feedings for her soul because she told me so.

I, too, would reap the benefits of my obedience. It's here that I learned more about listening to the voice of God. I also learned what discernment felt like. I knew when she needed a letter that would give her a much-needed laugh, just as I knew when she needed a message filled with scripture and doctrine: a letter to remind her of his presence, no matter the circumstance. And there were times when God instructed me to write her letters specific to her battle with Cancer.

My eyes drew big when I came across a letter dated January 24, 2022. The letter talked about a time I sat at the back of the van next to my cousin, a prophetess. We had traveled down to Trenton, New Jersey, to fellowship with our affiliate church, New Holy Cross. The ride home always called for a need to loosen up a few buttons to get comfy for the long haul back down. I watched my cousin unloosen the white clergy tab that sat fastened in place tightly around her neck. The tab represents a consecration to God, one's dedication to one's religious calling, and public profession of faith. And these tabs are typically set aside for individuals serving in the capacity of leadership: Pastors, Ministers, Apostles, Elders, and so on.

My eyes stayed focused on her clergy tab as my curiosity asked her if I could hold the tab in my hand. The moment felt sacred. I lifted the tab up near my neck as I caught a glimpse of myself in the mirror while the future ran through my mind; I wondered if one day God would use me in such a capacity that allowed me to wear the tab, too.

I could feel the tears drawing near to my eyes as I continued to stare at the letter, knowing pastor would be proud. Proud, but not surprised because she already told me that one day, I would indeed be an evangelist. And now she wasn't here to see the moment, but in hindsight, she saw the moment before I did.

My pastor passed away on January 26, 2023. The moment felt identical to my mother's transition. Heart-breaking, but yet part peace-filling. I felt empty yet full of God's promise. I'd sit in the hallway asking God for supernatural healing, a miraculous shift in her prognosis, but like my mother – he touched her with his ultimate healing while she rested in a warm bed awaiting his arrival.

Hours before her passing, I stood by her bedside, touching the side of her face to let my presence be known.

"Sister Von," she whispered softly. I flexed my arm, making a muscle, and offered her a reassuring reminder: "You're strong." She smiled in response, confirming the gesture; my spirit bore witness that God was indeed with her, surrounding her with his presence.

I left the hospital that day carrying her strength and every word that she's ever taught me about Jesus. Each prayer that she's ever petitioned to the heaven's on my behalf and every revelation that she graciously shared with me throughout the years. I cherished those special moments, holding them close to my heart like a precious badge of honor.

Just a few months after her passing, my pastor's prophecy about me amazingly came to fruition. Notably, I had previously received the same vision from another pastor years before her prophecy. In 2019, yet another pastor, whom I barely knew, spoke similar words over me, but when God called me into evangelism, I had no choice but to tell him yes.

He reinforced his calling by highlighting precise moments, dates, and times that had been part of my preparation all along.

Like that warm afternoon back in 2005, it remains a vivid memory today. I'd been hustling around at work to finish my paperwork before the deadline came chasing after me. Fifteen cases, several home visits still left to complete, return phone calls to make- a bit overwhelming for a Friday. Nonetheless, my heart still stretched long for the families I worked with. The life of a case manager was never quiet and polite. I had promised a parent to stop by on a home visit to review documents she received from the Department of Youth and Family Services. Months ago, she confided in me about her struggles with reading, which left her uneasy about signing important documents.

I confirmed the documents to be in order as I handed her a pen. "Sign here. It's okay for you to add your signature," I told her. She thanked me for taking the time out to do this favor while placing her hand on a bible nearby. She opened the bible and stared at the pages as if she were all alone.

"I can't read, but I can understand the bible," she said with gratitude. She went on to talk about God and his goodness despite times of struggle. As professionals serving in the field of social work, we are trained to be culturally competent; however, we do not initiate conversations based on religion to avoid imposing our own values and beliefs on families.

I continued to let her speak voluntarily.

"I have been going to church since a little girl. It's the only thing I really know," she continued.

I could see her eyes holding unspoken memories, transporting her back to her childhood; I sat quietly,. as she took the ride. I bet she could still smell the scent of old, worn wooden pews and Grandma's peppermints. White dress shoes, and thick white stockings on Easter Sunday. Monday night bible study, Tuesday night children's church, Wednesday night choir rehearsal; I wondered if she attended the same church as Steve Harvey? And let's not forget the other three services that were leading up to Sunday.

However, I couldn't relate. I grew up going to church only on Christmas, Easter, and Mother's Day.

Our conversation ended with her telling me to trust God, even when life doesn't make sense. Her story is a testament to her faith! Unable to read, yet receiving God's blessing of wisdom to grasp the depths of the bible.

I drove off, encouraged by her story, while pondering my own. It seemed almost immediately that God had me read the book of Ezekiel chapter two. I hadn't read or heard this bible verse before- in fact, I barely read any verse from the bible. But something tugged on me on that day to read the chapter. From what I gathered, God was preparing Ezekiel to go to a group of people who were stubborn and rebellious. He told Ezekiel to deliver a specific word about repentance even if the people refused to listen. I kept that thought tucked away in my back pocket but later lost it in the wash on laundry day.

After having that one memory, the rest of them fell in line like dominoes. God began to show me more moments, times, and dates. The relationships I was in, the dreams I was having, being a witness to my mother pray to God, Grandma's candy box, my bout with anxiety, the encounter I had at my Aunt Darlene's house with my cousin, the falling out with certain people: all of it being a preparation all along.

In 2023, following the passing of my pastor, I publicly announced my call to evangelism during my church hour of prayer, fulfilling the wisdom Pastor Sawyer had shared with me to "just tell the Lord yes."

So, exactly what is evangelism, one might ask? Evangelism is the act of sharing the Christian gospel. It consists of spreading the message and teaching of Jesus Christ. An evangelist is a disciple who goes out into the world to promote the word of God with much faith that others will draw near to Jesus as well. That's the broad concept of it. And let me add this here: all believers of Christ are evangelists based on the great commission where Jesus commands his followers to "go and make disciples of all nations." This is discussed in the book of Matthew, 28: 18-20. However, there are people whom God calls on specifically to be ordained into Evangelism as a vocation. People like me, for instance! They are set apart to go into specific regions, communities, and groups to share the gospel.

That's what my "yes" to God was about: embracing the mission that he was preparing me for.

Saying yes to Jesus is a part of our faith journey and a part of how we build a trusting relationship with him. At the time of my "yes," I didn't know exactly what my yes was for; however, I trusted God, and because I trusted in him, I knew it was for something abundant. Behold, he blessed me with the gift of Evangelism, a thought that dwelled way beyond my comprehension.

A few days before my trial sermon, God continued to show me the path that guided me right up to his door of Evangelism. He showed me a life that was scattered about in a million different pieces- beautifully formed together like a puzzle. The moment was complete, the picture was clear- I understood the assignment. I understood that I would be like Ezekiel and go into places to share the gospel, even when some didn't want to hear it. I was also commissioned to return to those who I once shared the same views with about God and tell them the genuine truth about him. Some of the conversations weren't easy as those topics were about sin; however, the reminder about God's saving grace always produced hope.

On the day of my trial sermon, I was dressed in all white, just as God had shown me in a dream many years ago. My topic to the church would hold remnants of Ezekiel chapter two. Some may call it a coincidence, some may call it a happenstance, but I call it God's Plan!

Don't Judge a Book by Its Cover

After my trial sermon, I noticed that my Journey to Christ grew to be the center of conversation when I hung out with loved ones and friends. And not to say that we never discussed God before, but it was evident that some of them were trying to figure out my newfound identity in Christ.

For instance, I was sitting with a friend one day when she asked me, "Wow, you gave your life to Christ!" As she talked, I could still feel the cool of the water embracing my skin from the day of baptism. But I could also sense her hesitation. I knew she had more questions to ask me. I could see the dialogue forming on the tip of her tongue, getting ready for dismount. That's when she looked at me with a mix of curiosity and caution and asked, "Are you still gay?"

I remember thinking about why she asked me this question. Was it my "tomboy" appearance that pushed her into the assumption that I was still gay? Or was it the mere fact that I hadn't pursued a relationship with a man to prove my exile from homosexuality? And then, there's that theory that some believe, once gay, always gay!

One thing for certain about homosexuality is this; it has caused much controversy both in and out of the church. I believe much of this controversy stems from its ambiguity: it's unclear and confusing for some people; furthermore, it's interpreted in so many ways both in and out of the church. And even though God provides us with very clear details and context about homosexuality, the complexity of this topic remains an ongoing debate amid society.

These debates are driven by the various dimensions, angles, and sides to homosexuality: it's multifaceted. For example, debating homosexuality as it applies to God's healing and deliverance. This is a topic that we can debate until the cows come home. These debates are sometimes influenced by tradition and one's perception of homosexuality. What we think deliverance should look like and what tradition says deliverance should look like.

God gave me a clearer understanding of healing and deliverance during a time when I least expected it. I was at home on a typical weekday night. My body sank into the soft cushions of my couch as the evening crept in. Wrapped snugly in the warmth of my favorite comforter, I surrendered to a night of chill: binge-watching TV series, enjoying some of my favorite snacks, and roaming aimlessly through Facebook and TikTok. No plans, no agenda- just me hanging out on a cold winter night, waiting for a good time to unfold on its own. YouTube streaming in the background from my TV, sound being drowned out by the noise I made from watching funny reels and reading posts on Facebook out loud. My go to when I was overdue for a much-needed laugh, where ridiculous memes, funny posts from friends, and hilarious videos sat just one scroll away. And on this night, the community was on a roll.

As the laughter died down, my gaze drifted back to the TV, where I checked to see if anything new had popped up on the channel. YouTube's algorithm had wandered so far from my original playlist it somehow landed on a podcast titled "With the Peerys." I turned the volume up and became immediately drawn to the woman talking on the screen. Something about her was very intriguing. She spoke with such articulation.

Her demeanor was cool, her style of dress artsy; she's dope, I thought to myself as she fiddled with her dreads that rested beneath her baseball cap. She had this swag about her that quite honestly reminded me, well- I guess of me! Was it the gap in her teeth that drew the resemblance or the oversized sweatshirt that matched my fly? Whatever it was, I connected with her! She held a spirit of compassion that exuded through the screen with ease and a great sense of humor that invited me closer to the TV.

She sat next to her husband, which grabbed my attention even more. This woman that looked like a "tomboy" had a husband? I watched the couple fire jokes back and forth throughout the segment, which kept the conversation balanced.

Funny people, I thought! I didn't know them at all, but for some reason, I felt proud of them. I was looking at two young disciples glimmering in an authentic love for God; it was evident; you could feel it and hear it blast off like love letters in the words they spoke. And for that, I was proud.

In this particular segment, the wife, Jackie, spoke about homosexuality. This is a topic that has been the main event lately on many other podcasts. However, her conveyance was different. She spoke about this topic in a manner that gave biblical language, comprehension, expression, and explanation of what a person really feels when experiencing battles with identity and sexual orientation.

Her message provided more than a "just pray"! And she didn't stop there- she spoke about sin in general as it applies to every kind of sinful nature. Her conversation was inclusive of all struggles. I sat back, listening closely while wishing I had come across her podcast before my friend asked me if I was still gay.

The more she spoke, the more I grew excited because it felt like, finally, someone was getting me. And finally, someone understands my go-through, and it's all backed with great context. She had the biblical knowledge and theology to better explain to people what healing and deliverance from homosexuality actually look like. Not only did she have the wisdom and biblical understanding to deliver a message with such divine power, but she also experienced these moments personally.

She understood what it felt like to have been gay, loved God, and be called into discipleship all at the same time.

I dedicated my binge-watch time to some of her other podcasts and different shows that she made appearances on. Throughout my indulgence, I discovered something beautiful. And Colorful! This discovery brought me Joy. It relieved me from the pressures and burdens that were beginning to weigh me down. The moment felt destined, and I was thankful to God for his timing. The moment blessed me with the answers I, too, had questioned about healing and deliverance from homosexuality.

The answers sat in the undertones of her cadence that spoke to me like poetry. And it sat there with much patience, gentleness, and love. It whispered: Holiness! That's what deliverance looks like! Deliverance from homosexuality looks like HOLINESS. Jackie had a great point, and I agreed with her God-giving concept.

But what's Holiness? It means to live our lives in a way that reflects God's glory rather than conforming to the ways of the world.

While holiness sits at the base of deliverance, some of us, saved and unsaved, base deliverance on appearance. The problem with this is that outward appearances cannot reflect one's inner spiritual transformation accurately. So, where did we learn to have these superficial perspectives? Had to be social media! Maybe church tradition has played a part. Lastly, culture has an impact on how we see things. And if we are not careful, these outlets can cause a wedge between our freedom in experiencing God. Wow, right? And these wedges are capable of manifesting in very subtle ways. For example, going back to the question that my friend asked me: Are you still gay?

It didn't matter that I professed my love for Christ. And that I sat before a multitude of people to be baptized. And that I had not been in a relationship with a woman for several years. Or that I spread the gospel to people with whom I cross paths with. Or that I fast every Tuesday and that I spend countless hours with Jesus. I can go on and on about my journey to Christ.

However, those factors don't really matter to people who feel like "deliverance from homosexuality" should look a certain way. What my friend really wanted to say to me was, "If you're no longer gay, then you should be in a relationship with a man and should be having some children real soon. Until then, you're still gay"! That's a great example of how tradition can sound; also a great example that shows the pressures that tradition can place on individuals who have left the lifestyle of homosexuality.

Those are the wedges that will try to sit in between one's freedom and experiencing God. As a follower of Christ, I once carried those burdens. I spent plenty of time questioning my deliverance, even after knowing that God had transformed me. That's because I was basing my deliverance on tradition, not on holiness.

I was hard on myself for not meeting the markers and expectations of tradition. I didn't feel delivered because, as a woman, I didn't wear heels, I didn't put on makeup, and I sure didn't want to put on a dress! And a relationship with a man, well, that thought was hard to comprehend altogether.

However, watching "With the Peerys" gave me an "Aha moment": That sudden realization, insight, and discovery that our focus should be holiness: living our lives in a way that reflects God's glory rather than conforming to the ways of the world. Surrendering all of ourselves to God, including our desires!

This "aha moment" allowed me to understand that deliverance from homosexuality differs from person to person and that God's healing is not always cookie-cutter. We are unique; he deals with us and handles us in different manners, making our transformation a journey of our own.

When I chose to live a life surrendered to Christ, it wasn't just about walking away from a lifestyle, but it was about walking into something greater: holiness, identity, and purpose in him. This decision brought many layers to it, especially in how I understood relationships and sexuality.

Some who turn from same-sex relationships may eventually enter into a God-led heterosexual marriage. Others may choose abstinence, meaning they refrain from sexual activity for a season or until marriage. Then there are those, like myself, who are walking in celibacy—for now. For me, this means living unmarried and abstinent, fully focused on God, and allowing him to shape every area of my life.

Celibacy may be a lifelong calling for some, and for others, like me, it may be the season I'm in as I continue to walk closely with God. If he leads me into a marriage one day, it will be because it aligns with his purpose for my life. But whether it's for a season or a lifetime, my heart remains surrendered.

Knowing the difference between abstinence and celibacy is very important, as abstinence is often temporary or situational. It's something someone may practice while waiting for God's direction. Celibacy, on the other hand, oftentimes is a longer commitment—a sacred space of devotion to God that allows for clarity, healing, and deeper intimacy with him.

Choosing a holy life isn't about fitting into a mold or proving anything. It's about letting God do the transforming. And through that, I've found freedom, not in becoming something I wasn't, but in becoming more of who he created me to be.

There's a misconception that surrendering to Christ is all about what you can't do. As if choosing holiness is just a list of restrictions and religion. But the truth is, this isn't about being on a "do not do" list for God. This is about being called into a life that I never knew I could live, a life full of peace, wholeness, joy, and strength.

Yes, I once lived differently. And no, I didn't walk away from the lifestyle because I was forced, broken down, or manipulated. I walked away because I met Jesus, and he gave me something more. People may think this is just a phase or that I'm suppressing who I used to be, but what some don't understand is that I've been transformed. I'm not grieving what I left behind. I'm rejoicing in what I've found.

I didn't say "no" to myself because I was pressured into it. I said "yes" to Christ because I encountered his love. That love reshaped my identity, not into a shell of myself, but into a woman who now knows who she really is. I don't live in confusion. I live in confidence, not in me, but in the one who strengthens me.

I get to walk in purpose. I get to love fully and purely. I get to be free, not just from sin, but from opinions, labels, and lies. I can do all things through Christ, not because I'm trying hard to be something I'm not, but because he lives in me.

Am I perfect? No, I'm not! We all experience temptation; it's a part of humanity. However, by keeping holiness as the goal while walking in Christ, it's easier to turn and walk away from sinful nature. And holiness is something that should stretch across all factors in our lives, not just as it applies to sexuality. God should come first in everything we do!

I pray that this chapter has given you more clarity to those who may question what transpires in a person who no longer lives a lifestyle of homosexuality. Like any person who gives their life to Christ, a process of transformation and sanctification happens. And that process can look different for everyone. Our job as a people is to uplift and love one another, not to judge a book by its cover, as outward appearances don't always reflect what's going on within.

Happy New Year

Resting beneath my blanket that kept me warm all night, my eyes looked out to the brand-new day. No clock around, but the feel of the soft morning suggested 7am. The quiet of the room wrapped around me like a hug, soothing my thoughts without interruption. I lay there thinking about life in general. I thought about the presence of God's favor hovering over me as of late. And I specifically remember this morning because it was New Year's Eve. That fast, three-hundred-and-sixty-five days had run through the year like a track star. But ever-so-grateful, I said my prayers to God and soon after exited the warmth of my California king. It wasn't long before I noticed bags of laundry sitting in the corner of my room, waiting to be washed.

As a young adult, somewhere, I learned that if I wanted to have good luck in the New Year, then eating black-eyed peas and washing my clothes was a must.

I recall eating spoons of black-eyed eyed-peas and doing laundry up until the last-minute chasing prosperity. I also remember masking beans with ketchup to hide the bitterness that stood so bold in the beans that touched my tongue. But I have come a long way since following superstitious rituals during the New Year season.

I've found my freedom in knowing that my prosperity and blessings manifest through Jesus Christ! It's not some made-up superstition that holds no truth or weight behind it. Stuff like, if you see a black cat, turn around and head in the opposite direction, or break a mirror, and you're doomed for seven years. I was free from all of these crazy superstitions but also free from using the word "luck." With that in mind, I shoved my unwashed clothes into the closet and shut the door.

My day grew instantly free, giving me more time to prepare for service at Agape Worship Center. This church came to mind right after my pastor announced the closing of our church for watch night service. Instead, we were invited to a fellowship with our sister church, Gethsemane Temple, in Plainfield, NJ.

A lot of history stands behind this great church as it travels way back to the early 1900's. I wasn't around then, but I'm told that people came to this church by the busload just to be in the presence of the Lord. They'd come together on weekdays and weekends to sing old hymns while saints tarried on in the spirit. Most of their services were said to be more like revivals; people were actually renewed after visiting Gethsemane.

This is the same church where some of my family members planted their roots in Jesus and found spiritual guidance as well. Aunt Becky and Uncle Roy- my Aunt Shirl too; all have passed on, but their connection to this church began back in the mid-eighties.

At the present time, my bloodline still runs through this church. One is my pastor! It's his home church, the church where his place in ministry was prophesied over his life as a little boy. Right at the same altar, his late Mother, Pastor Staci D. Sawyer, found her faith.

Oftentimes, he also referenced the revivals that took place at Gethsemane. I bet memories still play vividly in his spirit as tears draw near sometimes when he relives the moments of singing old hymns and spirituals.

The nostalgia at this church remains a remnant today, even in the order of worship. You could hear and feel the tradition of the church still linger through the sanctuary.

For me, I could feel the tradition of the church in the dress I put on each time I was there to fellowship. Women entering the sanctuary were expected to wear a dress, somewhat of a rule that was practiced.

I now own five dresses because of Gethsemane Temple! And I must add that wearing dresses has never been something of my interest, lol! And I love this church, but the thought of wearing a dress to bring my New Year in troubled my spirit. It troubled me enough to ponder visiting another church, like Agape, a church where worship is known to be less traditional. And it wasn't about the wearing of the dress itself, but it was more about me learning to be unapologetically me!

I wanted to feel relaxed, wearing sweatpants or jeans- or maybe a good pair of sneakers if that's what I decided.

My heart desired it. I was also ready to fellowship amongst new faces and experience praise and worship in a way that I hadn't experienced in a long time. I wanted to hear contemporary gospel songs and dance to beats that encompassed the musician's uniqueness.

However, my plans were altered during my noonday hour of prayer. The church fellowship invitation, which had seemed like a warm gesture, turned out to be a pastoral assignment for our church. So, in other words, I was expected to be there. And I've been on assignments before. It's all a part of my spiritual calling and service to God.

When we are called, we go, even if it means to stand in as a support to the congregation. But I felt torn. I was heavily clothed in a desire to visit Agape, but I also wanted to remain committed to my church.

After my hour of prayer, I prayed some more, seeking divine wisdom to guide me through the conflicting desires and uncertainties I felt within.

During my time of prayer, I thought about a song that my friend David sent to me just a few days prior. We live 5,000 miles apart, but our spirits still dance in harmony. From the moment our words met on social media, an unspoken connection has kept us together for the past four years. And since our union, David has walked right along with me on my journey to Christ, sending me profound messages, prayers, and songs. It feels like God uses him to speak to me. I can honestly say there's something very divine about our bond.

But going back to the song, David sent me a track titled "Deeper," sung by Marvin Sapp. As I played the track, the sound of the piano's gentle melody began to speak to my heart as he sang:

There is a call
That resounds in my ear
It's calling me deeper
Breaks every failure and removes all my fears
It's calling me deeper
See the place that I'm in
Can no longer contain my destiny
And this growth has its pain
But I adhere to the call inside of me

169

The song instantly became my anthem for the next few hours as it ministered to me about the exact uncertainties that sat within. From the rhythm of keyboards to the sound of the drums, overlapped with subtle plucking from the bass guitar and strings, my spirit encountered an atmosphere of inspiration. The lyrics empowered me to break free from limitations, leaving tradition behind in order to reach new spiritual heights and connection with God. I understood the assignment!

Despite my desire to attend Agape Worship Center, I chose to fellowship with Gethsemane for the New Year. However, I was going under one condition! I planned to wear whatever clothing made me feel comfortable.

The nine o'clock hour showed up like a thief in the night. It was time to head to Gethsemane for their watch night service. I pulled out my sweat suit and sneakers-grabbed my bible, and headed to Plainfield.

The thirty-minute ride became a mental movie reel, replaying vivid memories of moments from my previous New Year's Eve celebrations. One year, I remember friends giving me milk to help cleanse my system of all the alcohol I had consumed.

Another year, I remember spending hundreds of dollars just to look fashionable for a few hours. I thought about the clubs, the lounges, and bars that I had been in and out of over the years, God covering me through each escapade.

But on this night, for several years straight, I can say that God created in me a clean heart and renewed the right spirit in me. This thought alone nudged my hand to turn the volume up to the max level to replay my anthem song, "Deeper." I must have driven to the church on autopilot.

Entering the sanctuary with tears flowing internally, I had no words; it was just me in the moment with God. I didn't know exactly what I was feeling as I sat in the middle pew, but I discerned that something divine was happening within. I could feel it stirring in my soul. My silent cries began to flow outwardly as they morphed into a weep that felt like a release. God began to speak to my heart. He whispered, "Go"!

I had only been at Gethsemane for about fifteen minutes, but without hesitation, I gathered my Bible and hustled back to my truck. I knew where God was sending me. I arrived at Agape Worship Center about twenty minutes before the New Year entered. The usher found the last seat on the side of the aisle I was on. It seemed like the chair was waiting just for me.

The sanctuary's atmosphere resonated with fulfilling the desires I had about my night of worship. I told the Lord thank you. Flags were suspended in the air, representing countries from across the world.

People from all cultural backgrounds filled the large room dressed in an array of attire. My attire fitted right in! White, Black, Asian, Hispanic, Latin; the church was alive, free of mundane.

A diverse crowd of followers gathered in one space, the commonality being to celebrate Jesus. What a beautiful way to begin the year with faith, hope, and community.

Though missing the praise and worship team, my spirit still danced with joy as I prepared myself to hear from Evangelist Shandra Riley. Her powerful voice filled the distance of the whole venue as she looked upon us and said:

> Unexpected moving! Divine intervention is way beyond logic. Don't worry about how he's going to do it. Just watch him do it; God's got a plan. Things will manifest in 2025 that God already planned in 2024. Mind-blowing manifestation! Declare boldly! Get ready for stronger faith. Start seeing it now. You don't have to explain anything to anyone. Keep your eyes on Jesus. Believe in the Lord!

As I reflected on my journey, the message echoed a truth that has walked with me since the very beginning of my walk with Christ. No matter what obstacles I have faced in life so far, God has been there, walking with me like footsteps in the sand, intervening and interceding on my behalf. Picking me up when I fell down and teaching me when I just didn't know any better. Correcting my mistakes and helping me to live life with humility.

Over the last nine years, God has healed me in places where I was broken. And this year, he has given me the strength to Unpack My Luggage!

Be you and let God do the rest

God Bless!

Conclusion

I thank you for taking the time to read Unpacked Luggage. I pray that my book has served as insightful and inspiring to your own relationship with Jesus. The purpose of releasing this book was to depict how much God loves us, no matter our circumstances. Gay, straight, rich, poor, black, white, democrat or republican, Jesus will for us is Holiness, and it's his power that brings us to his will!

While millions of people know the name Jesus and even believe who he is, some have never been saved. If you are that person and you want to be saved, today is your day. Today is your day to commit yourself to Jesus through reading his prayer of salvation:

That if thou shalt confess with thy mouth the Lord Jesus, and shalt believe in thine heart that God hath raised him from the dead, thou shalt be saved. For with the heart, man believeth unto righteousness; and with the mouth, confession is made unto salvation.
—Romans 10: 9-10

You are saved!

About the Author

Business owner Chyvonne Thomas was born and raised in Edison, "Potters Crossing," New Jersey, to the Late Linda Thomas and Williams Thomas Jr. She attended the Edison School System. In 1996, she moved to Roselle, NJ, where she graduated from Abraham Clark High School.

She graduated from Rutgers University in 2003, earning a dual degree in Psychology and Criminal Justice. Upon her graduation, she dedicated eighteen years of service to the field of social work before opening her own business, PLR Motivational Speaking and Resources Unlimited, in 2020. Her organization is committed to providing services to enhance the lives of kids and young adults.

The Acronym P.L.R is a dedication to her Late Grandmother Parthenia, Linda, and Richard Thomas. She chose P.L.R. as these three individuals helped lay the foundation for her to reach the platforms that she is reaching today.

Chyvonne is a Member of New Life Ministries of South Edison, where she is the President of the Street Team and Youth Department. Through this form of Ministry, she enjoys spreading the love of Jesus Christ and bringing hope to the community.

In her spare time, she enjoys spending time with her family, known as the "ThomasNation," and hanging out with her brother, William Thomas, and sister, Alicia Thomas.

Glossary

Innate immunity: Existing in, belonging to, or determined by factors present in an individual from birth.

Conscious learning: Being engaged in the learning process.

Unconscious learning: Learning without awareness, regardless of what sort of learning is being acquired.

Unorthodox: Contrary to what is usual, traditional, or accepted; not orthodox.

Empathy: Being aware of and sharing another person's feelings, experiences, and emotions.

Sanctification: The action of making or declaring something holy.

Oxytocin: Associated with trust, sexual arousal, and relationship-building

U-Hauling: Refers to the idea that lesbians tend to move in together after a short period of time of being together.

Discern: Perceive or recognize something.

Digress: To turn aside, especially from the main subject of attention of the course of argument.

Elder: One of a plurality of biblically qualified men who jointly shepherd and oversee a local body of believers.

Evangelist: A person who seeks to convert others to the Christian faith, especially by public preaching.

Will: What God ideally wants.

Perplexity: A state of confusion or a complicated and difficult situation or thing.

Concoction: A mixture of various ingredients or elements.

Still waters: Restful water or deep peace.

Emotional stronghold: Those very things that stand in the way of your relationship with God and being what he created you to be.

Superstitious rituals: A belief or practice or practice resulting from ignorance, fear of the unknown, trust in magic or chance, or false conception of causation.

Baptism: The immersion of a believer in water in the name of the Father, the Son, and the Holy Spirit.

Metaphor: A figure of speech in which a word or phrase is applied to an object or action to which it is not literally applicable.

Exodus: A mass departure.

Purge: To cleanse of guilt and sin, to remove impurities by cleaning, to become pure, clean, or clear.

Pruning: To remove any fleshly attitudes or behaviors that are still hanging on from before we were saved.

Flock: Those who are led and taught.

Clergy Tab: Symbolization and dedication to God and one's religious duties.

Consecration: Fully surrendered to the Lord and his plans.

Transformation: A change of one's nature or a change at the heart of who a person is.

Holiness: To live our lives in a way that reflects God's glory rather than conforming to the ways of the world.

Congregation: A group of people assembled for religious worship.

Manifest: To make openly known; appear.

Prosperity: To have continued success, to thrive, grow, flourish, and have wealth and good fortune.

Fellowship: Common sharing of the grace and of the blessings of God.

Revival: A return to God through confession and repentance.

Tarry: To sit down quietly before God and wait.

Hymns: A religious song or Psalm.

Remnant: What is left over.

Tradition: The handing down of statements, beliefs, legends, customs, and information.

Sanctuary: Holy place where God is present.

Unapologetically: Without expressing regret.

Escapade: An act of incident involving excitement, daring, or adventure.

Anthem: A rousing or uplifting song identified with a particular group, body, or cause.

Autopilot: Doing something without thinking about it or without making an effort.

Divine: Relating to or coming directly from God.

Morphed: The outward expression of an inner essence.

Humility: Seeking to bring glory and honor to God and looking out for the interests of others.

References

- Tupac Shakur: The Rose That Grew through Concrete

- Bustle.com: U-Haul Syndrome

- C.S Lewis- (YouTube) The Clear difference between God's Voice and your thoughts.

- C.S Lewis- Mere Christianity

- Video of Dad Facebook @chyvonnethomas

- Phaedrus- https://harveymackayacademy.com/thinkgs-are-not-as-as-they-perceive-them-to-be/

- Frost, Robert. "The Road not Taken." The Poetry of Robert Frost, edited by Edward Connery Lathem, Henry Holt. 1979 pp. 15-16

- Peek Motivation: Youtube.com: Dr. Myles reveals: If you wake up between 3am and 5am.

- Cast Away was released in 2000

- Story of Joseph Genesis Chapter 40-50

- Jackie Hill Perry (YouTube)- With the Perrys